Palm Pre
The Missing Manual
First Edition

Palm Pre: The Missing Manual

By Edward C. Baig

Copyright © 2009 Edward C. Baig. All rights reserved.
Printed in Canada.

Published by O'Reilly Media, Inc., 1005 Gravenstein Highway North, Sebastopol, CA 95472.

O'Reilly books may be purchased for educational, business, or sales promotional use. Online editions are also available for most titles (safari.oreilly.com). For more information, contact our corporate/institutional sales department: 800.998.9938 or corporate@oreilly.com.

Editor: Peter McKie

Production Editor: Nellie McKesson

Indexer: Fred Leise

Cover Designers: Randy Comer, Karen Montgomery, and Suzy Wiviott

Interior Designer: Ron Bilodeau

Print History:

August 2009:   First Edition.

ISBN: 9780596803704

[F]

Contents

Part 2: Getting in Touch with Others

Chapter 4

Chapter 5

Part 3: Going Online

Chapter 6

Chapter 7

Part 4: Music, Video, and Images

Part 5: Appendixes

The Missing Credits

About the Author

Edward C. Baig (author) is is the weekly Personal Tech columnist for *USA Today* and a contributor of tech trend pieces in the newspaper and at usatoday.com. He is co-host of *USA Today*'s Talking Tech podcast and a weekly contributor to ABC News' Tech Bytes, which appears on ABC TV affiliates around the country and at *www.abcnews.go.com/technology*. He is the author of recent editions of *Macs For Dummies* and co-author of *iPhone For Dummies*. Before joining USA Today in 1999, Ed was on staff at *Business Week*, *U.S. News & World Report*, and *Fortune* magazines. He is passionate about music, politics, and all sports, especially his beloved New York Giants. Contact him at *edbaig@gmail.com*.

About the Creative Team

Peter McKie (editor) is an editor at Missing Manuals. He was graduated from Boston University's School of Journalism and lives in New York City, where he researches the history of old houses and, every once in a while, sneaks into abandoned buildings. Email: *pmckie@gmail.com*.

Dawn Frausto (editor) is assistant editor for the Missing Manual series. When not working, she plays soccer, beads, and causes trouble. Email: *dawn@oreilly.com*.

Nellie McKesson (production editor) is a graduate of St. John's College in Santa Fe, New Mexico. She lives in Brighton, Mass., and spends her spare time making t-shirts for friends (mattsaundersbynellie.etsy.com). Email: *nellie@oreilly.com*.

Jan Jue (copy editor) enjoys freelance copyediting, a good mystery, and the search for the perfect pot sticker.

Fred Leise (indexer) provides consulting services in taxonomy design, and indexes books and journals in a variety of fields. Slightly Auspergian, he loves small, repetitive motions, which is probably why he is an avid knitter. Email: *fredleise@contextualanalysis.com*.

Will Honey (technical reviewer) is a Palm Pre fanatic and an administrator of and avid poster to the Palm Pre Forum (*www.palmpreforum.org*). He has written several reviews for Pre-based products and publishes them on the forum. You can contact him there as Tibfib.

Jesus Novoa (technical reviewer) is a computer technology student at NJIT. He's a fan of new music, so he often listens to Pandora when out with his Palm Pre. Jesus travels to Japan every few years, and associates with many indie Japanese bands. You can usually find him in New York City's indie music venues, checking out (or hanging out with) bands.

Acknowledgments

This book would not have been possible without the creative people at O'Reilly Media whose names appear on the previous page, as well as those at O'Reilly who toil under the radar. You have my full appreciation.

Special thanks are in order to my especially talented editors Peter McKie and Dawn Frausto for their dogged pursuit of excellence and for guiding this Missing Manual newbie through the entire process. I also wish to thank Peter Meyers for trusting me with this project. Technical reviewers Will Honey and Jesus Novoa made sure I didn't miss anything and were responsible for uncovering several of the tips you'll read in this book.

I'm especially grateful to Palm Inc.'s Paul Cousineau, Matt Crowley, and Tina Hampton for diligently and thoroughly answering my queries at all hours of the day and night and on weekends. You were all quite simply a pleasure to deal with. Several other people at Palm deserve thanks: Lynn Fox, Jon Zilber, Leslie Letts, Wendy Collier, Michael Leslie, Margarita Roehricht, Kristin Schwarz, Caroline Bressler, Paul Araquistain, and Lally Narwal.

At Sprint, I'd like to thank David Owens, Mark J. Elliott, and Stephanie Vinge-Walsh.

Thanks also to my *USA Today* colleagues Jim Henderson, Geri Tucker, and Nancy Blair for supporting this project. I also appreciate the guidance provided by my agent, Matt Wagner.

Mostly I want to thank my amazing family—Janie, Sydney, Sammy, and my "canine son" Eddie Jr. You gave me love and kept me (somewhat) sane through the long hours. Thanks for understanding why I was all-too-frequently at the keyboard working and not spending more time with you. I love you always.

—Edward C. Baig

The Missing Manual Series

Missing Manuals are witty, superbly written guides to computer products that don't come with printed manuals (which is just about all of them). Each book features a handcrafted index; cross-references to specific pages (not just chapters); and RepKover, a detached-spine binding that lets the book lie perfectly flat without the assistance of weights or cinder blocks.

Recent and upcoming titles include:

Access 2007: The Missing Manual by Matthew MacDonald

AppleScript: The Missing Manual by Adam Goldstein

AppleWorks 6: The Missing Manual by Jim Elferdink and David Reynolds

CSS: The Missing Manual, Second Edition, by David Sawyer McFarland

Creating a Web Site: The Missing Manual, Second Edition by Matthew MacDonald

David Pogue's Digital Photography: The Missing Manual by David Pogue

Dreamweaver 8: The Missing Manual by David Sawyer McFarland

Dreamweaver CS3: The Missing Manual by David Sawyer McFarland

Dreamweaver CS4: The Missing Manual by David Sawyer McFarland

eBay: The Missing Manual by Nancy Conner

Excel 2003: The Missing Manual by Matthew MacDonald

Excel 2007: The Missing Manual by Matthew MacDonald

Facebook: The Missing Manual by E.A. Vander Veer

FileMaker Pro 9: The Missing Manual by Geoff Coffey and Susan Prosser

FileMaker Pro 10: The Missing Manual by Susan Prosser and Geoff Coffey

Flash 8: The Missing Manual by E.A. Vander Veer

Flash CS3: The Missing Manual by E.A. Vander Veer and Chris Grover

Flash CS4: The Missing Manual by Chris Grover with E.A. Vander Veer

FrontPage 2003: The Missing Manual by Jessica Mantaro

Google Apps: The Missing Manual by Nancy Conner

The Internet: The Missing Manual by David Pogue and J.D. Biersdorfer

iMovie 6 & iDVD: The Missing Manual by David Pogue

iMovie '08 & iDVD: The Missing Manual by David Pogue

iMovie '09 & iDVD: The Missing Manual by David Pogue and Aaron Miller

iPhone: The Missing Manual, Second Edition by David Pogue

iPhoto '08: The Missing Manual by David Pogue

iPhoto '09: The Missing Manual by David Pogue and J.D. Biersdorfer

iPod: The Missing Manual, Seventh Edition by J.D. Biersdorfer and David Pogue

JavaScript: The Missing Manual by David Sawyer McFarland

Living Green: The Missing Manual by Nancy Conner

Mac OS X: The Missing Manual, Tiger Edition by David Pogue

Mac OS X: The Missing Manual, Leopard Edition by David Pogue

Microsoft Project 2007: The Missing Manual by Bonnie Biafore

Netbooks: The Missing Manual by J.D. Biersdorfer

Office 2004 for Macintosh: The Missing Manual by Mark H. Walker and Franklin Tessler

Office 2007: The Missing Manual by Chris Grover, Matthew MacDonald, and E.A. Vander Veer

Office 2008 for Macintosh: The Missing Manual by Jim Elferdink

Palm Pre: The Missing Manual by Ed Baig

PCs: The Missing Manual by Andy Rathbone

Photoshop Elements 7: The Missing Manual by Barbara Brundage

Photoshop Elements 6 for Mac: The Missing Manual by Barbara Brundage

PowerPoint 2007: The Missing Manual by E.A. Vander Veer

QuickBase: The Missing Manual by Nancy Conner

QuickBooks 2009: The Missing Manual by Bonnie Biafore

QuickBooks 2010: The Missing Manual by Bonnie Biafore

Introduction

At the January 2009 Consumer Electronics Show in Las Vegas, the executives from Palm Inc. were feeling the pressure. The company that created the pioneering Palm Pilot "personal digital assistant," was facing a skeptical press corps. The Pilot was a faded if fond memory, and Palm's once-darling Treo (until a few years ago the smartphone of choice for businesspeople) had grown tired next to Apple's iPhone and Research in Motion's ever-friendlier BlackBerry.

As a result, Palm's business was reeling. The product they were about to introduce would go a long way toward making or breaking the company.

That product, of course, was the Pre. And when the press conference ended, there was widespread agreement that Palm had unveiled something special, a pocket computer *extraordinaire*.

In designing the Pre, Palm borrowed many of the best elements of the iPhone while addressing some of its shortcomings—and adding a lot of its own mojo in the process (see Chapter 2's coverage of the Pre's multitasking talents, for example).

Where the iPhone offers an onscreen "virtual" keyboard, the Pre has a physical keyboard, a godsend if you've ever struggled with the iPhone's hit-or-miss keys.

When an iPhone's battery peters out, you have to find an Apple store for a replacement. Swapping out a spent battery in the Pre is as simple as opening the back and making the switch (and you can carry a spare with you just in case).

Photo-wise, the iPhone isn't so bright; it lacks a flash. The Pre includes a flash, so you never take a picture in the dark.

In most other respects, the Pre has all the makings of a state-of-the-art palm-sized PC: tilt and proximity sensors, access to fast phone and WiFi networks, GPS capability, and a slick music and video player.

Palm spent a lot of time thinking about the way you interact with the Pre, too. It has a fabulous new universal search feature that yields results the moment you start typing, and an interface that lets you switch among applications as though you were shuffling a deck of cards. And as befits any organizer from Palm, the Pre boasts a terrific calendar, address book, and task list.

The Pre has another unique feature: It's always connected to the Internet, reflecting Palm's belief in the emerging importance of the Web as a communications hub and access point for online programs. The smartphone puts that connection to good use with a clever organizing tool that Palm calls *Synergy*. Synergy collects and coordinates personal information—your contacts, email accounts, IM addresses, calendar appointments, and so on—from many sources over the Web and brings them together in one logical place—in a consolidated Contacts folder, for example, or in a single Email application that handles all your accounts. Chapter 3 has the details.

And if you need still more versatility, Palm built the Pre on a foundation of widely accepted programming standards. That means that individuals and companies can quickly create new applications—from multimedia tools to social networks. At the time this book was written, Palm still had a lot of catching up to do when it came to the App Catalog, where it sells these programs or makes them available for free (see Appendix B). The online store is still in a test phase, but its future looks bright.

Oh, and there's one more thing you shouldn't overlook: The Pre makes a darn good cellphone.

About This Book

Technology has come a long way through the years, but the same can't be said for instruction manuals. Many companies eschew printed instructions altogether or have moved user guides to inconvenient electronic PDF documents and/or the Internet. Even if you land in the right place, these materials don't exactly read like whodunits. And that's assuming you can read them at all. In some instances, manuals are poorly translated from another language or written by engineers for engineers.

The Palm Pre comes with a Get Started pamphlet and a Features guide, but these lack the depth, perspective, objectivity, and (when you need it most) the dab of humor you deserve. That's the purpose of this book—to serve as the manual that should have been in the box. In its pages, you'll find step-by-step instructions for every Pre feature and tips on how to get the most out of it. The pretty pictures sprinkled throughout help, too.

About the Outline

Palm Pre: The Missing Manual is divided into five parts:

- **Part 1, Getting to Know the Pre,** shows you around the design of the device, down to its buttons, controls, slick new interface, and navigational gestures.

- **Part 2, Getting in Touch with Others,** covers all things relating to phone calls, plus you'll learn to manage calendars, keep track of tasks, and jot down memos.

- **Part 3, Going Online,** tells you how to connect to cyberspace, browse the Web, and stay on top of email, text messaging, picture messaging, and instant messaging.

- **Part 4, Music, Video, and Images,** is about playing music, watching videos, and taking and admiring pictures.

- **Part 5, Appendixes,** includes helpful references for activating the phone, buying programs from the App Catalog, and finding fixes in the event that your Pre misbehaves.

About→These→Arrows

Throughout this book and the Missing Manual series, you'll find sentences like this one: "Go to the Calendar program's application menu, tap Preferences & Accounts→Default Event Duration, and then tap either 30 minutes or 2 hours. The arrows are simply shorthand for a *much* longer sequence of instructions, like this: "Open the Calendar's application menu and tap on the menu command "Preferences & Accounts". On the screen that pops up, tap the option "Default Event Duration", and then, on the next menu, tap either 30 minutes or 2 hours." Don't worry: This notation will make sense once you see it in action.

About MissingManuals.com

At *www.missingmanuals.com*, you'll find articles, tips, and updates to *Palm Pre: The Missing Manual*. In fact, we invite and encourage you to submit such corrections and updates yourself. In an effort to keep the book as up to date and accurate as possible, each time we print more copies, we'll make any confirmed corrections you've suggested. We'll also note such changes on the website, so you can mark important corrections in your own copy of the book if you like. (Go to *http://missingmanuals.com/feedback*, choose the book's name from the pop-up menu, and then click Go to see the changes.)

Also on our Feedback page, you can get expert answers to questions that come to you while reading this book, write a book review, and find groups for folks who share your interest in the Palm Pre. We'd love to hear your suggestions for new books in the Missing Manual line. There's a place for that on missingmanuals.com, too.

And while you're online, you can register this book at *www.oreilly.com* (you can jump directly to the registration page by going here: *http://tinyurl.com/yo82k3*). Registering means that we can send you updates about this book, and you'll be eligible for special offers like discounts on future editions of *Palm Pre: The Missing Manual.*

The Missing CD

As you read the book's chapters, you'll find references to websites that offer additional information. To get a neat, chapter-by-chapter list of all the materials cited here, head to the Missing CD page for this book. To get there, go to the Missing Manuals home page (*www.missingmanuals.com*), click the "Missing CD-ROMs" link on the left side, and then scroll down to *Palm Pre: The Missing Manual* and click the "Missing CD" link.

While you're on the Missing CD page, you can find updates to this book by clicking the link labeled "View Errata for this book" at the top of the page. You're invited and encouraged to submit corrections and updates, too. To do so, click the "Submit your own Errata" link.

Safari® Books Online

Safari Books Online   When you see a Safari® Books Online icon on the cover of your favorite technology book that means the book is available online through the O'Reilly Network Safari Bookshelf.

Safari offers a solution that's better than e-books. It's a virtual library that lets you easily search thousands of top tech books, cut and paste code samples, download chapters, and find quick answers when you need the most accurate, current information. Try it for free at *http://my.safaribooksonline.com*.

Chapter
1

Tour the Pre

I f you're like most Pre owners, you're more than ready to put your new phone to work. In fact, you probably already cracked the box, charged the battery, and started calling and texting friends. Who can blame you? The Pre's an alluring package.

But before you dive in much further, it's worth taking a few minutes to learn your way around. Throughout this book, and as long as you own your Pre, you'll need to know where things like the "gesture area" and the Quick Launch panel are, and what they do.

In this chapter, you'll discover what all the inviting buttons on the Pre do, take a look at the keyboard, tour the many parts of the touchscreen, and learn the basics of interacting with your new phone. So get ready—your tour's about to begin.

What Comes in the Box

If you haven't already pulled the Pre out of its handsome black-and-white box and peeked at its contents, here's the lowdown:

- **Get Started guide.** For a little fold-up pamphlet, this guide is surprisingly useful and worth keeping nearby, if only as a quickie reference to the finger movements, or *gestures* (see page 26), that help you navigate the Pre. The guide also shows you how to turn on, activate, and set up the Pre; open and move among applications (programs); and make a call, among other things. The guide comes in both English and Spanish versions.

- **Features guide.** If you hadn't already bought the Pre, you'd think this was an advertisement for most of the things you can do with it, including GPS navigation, Sprint TV, picture messaging, and more. This guide gives you a quick overview of how to get started with these and other applications.

- **License agreements, warranties, and safety and legal info.** Unless you're a lawyer, it's hard to imagine you'll actually take the time to read these disclaimers, not that it's a bad idea to look them over. (If you do read them, you'll learn—among other things—how Sprint calculates bills and that if you use third-party applications on the Pre, the application may collect or require Sprint to disclose your personal information.) And if the teeny-tiny type size is any indication, you're even less likely to read the warranty info that's included.

- **AC adapter and USB cable.** You use the AC adapter with the USB cableto recharge your Pre (see page 21). You also use the USB cable to sync files between thePre and your PC or Mac (see page 181), and even to connect to Apple's popular iTunes jukebox software to bring songs from your computer to the Pre (providing that option is still available; see the Note on page 182).

- **Stereo headset.** The standard-size (3.5mm) stereo headset has a switch on the cord for answering calls and a little microphone for getting your voice heard. And of course you can use the headset to listen to music or watch a video instead of piping those sounds through the Pre's built-in speaker. When you do so, the switch on the cord toggles between play and pause.

- **Pouch.** Your Pre is a beautiful little pocket computer. The soft black and (on the interior) orange pouch that's provided to keep it from getting dinged or scratched is functional, but isn't going to win any beauty con-tests. If style matters, you'll probably want to shop around for something that's better looking, perhaps even the leather case that Palm peddles as an accessory.

- **Recycling mailer.** Sprint includes a postage-paid pouch you can use to recycle the wireless phone you're replacing with your spiffy new Pre. It's an eco-friendly thing to do, and the proceeds from the program benefit a good cause, Internet safety for kids.

Set Up a Palm Profile

Before you can use your Pre, you have to set up what's called a "Palm Profile" on Palm's website. The Profile stores details about your Pre, your name and email address, and, more importantly, provides the following services:

- **Automatic backups.** Every day, Palm backs up your Pre, including applications you download from the App Catalog (see Appendix B). That means that if your Pre is ever lost, stolen, or damaged, your data is in a safe place and can be restored.

- **Updates.** From time to time, Palm fixes bugs or adds features to the Pre's operating system, which is called *webOS* (see page 5). When you have a Profile, Palm automatically downloads these updates to your Pre, though (within limits) you choose when to install them (see page 49).

- **Remote wipes.** If you ever lose your Pre, you can remotely erase all your personal information before the bad guys get it by logging into your Profile from another computer.

Setting up a Palm Profile is simple: When you turn on the phone for the first time, you see a series of screens that ask for your name, a password, the answer to a security question (like "What was your first car?" or "Where did your parents meet?"), and your email address. Palm uses this information to create your Profile and sends a verification message to the email address you entered. Open the email, click the link in it, and you've got yourself a Palm Profile.

You can change your profile info any time, either at the Palm Profile website (*http://tinyurl.com/kors3m*) or on the Pre itself (the Pre sends the updated info to the website). To change it on the Pre, go to the Launcher and tap Backup→Preferences→Palm Profile. Enter your password and then tap anything you want to change.

> **Tip** You can find links to all the websites mentioned in these pages on this book's Missing CD page at *www.missingmanuals.com*.

The Pre's New Foundation

Palm wanted the Pre to do almost everything that a desktop PC can do. Two of its requirements for the smartphone reflected that mindset: The Pre had to *multitask*—to run more than one program at a time (so you could surf the Web and get emails at the same time, for example)—and the Pre had to stay always connected to the Web, because most people use the Internet as part of their daily lives.

Palm succeeded on both counts. The Pre is a smartphone with impressive capabilities. But to let it do all that cool stuff, Palm needed a serious controlling program at the Pre's core (the program at the heart of every computer, including the Pre, is called the *operating system*). Since no multitasking, always-connected operating system existed for smartphones, Palm built its own, from the ground up. They called it *webOS*.

When you use your Pre, you don't interact directly with webOS, so you won't find a chapter devoted to it in this book. But it's good to know what webOS is, because it's responsible for nearly everything you do on the Pre—from multitasking to dynamically updating web pages and email inboxes. In addition, if you ever need to call customer support, representatives may refer to webOS, as may email messages from Palm.

The Pre from the Outside

The Pre's case looks sleek and seamless, but it houses a number of buttons, switches, and other components like the speaker, camera, and flash. It also houses the keyboard, one of the Pre's defining characteristics. This section looks at what you'll find on the outside of the Pre.

The Power Button

The Pre's power button curves around the upper-right corner of the phone's case.

It handles several tasks:

- **On/Off.** No surprise here: This button powers up and turns off your Pre. "Off" in this case means completely shut down—you can't make or receive calls or do anything but turn the Pre back on.

Power button   Ringer switch   Headphone Jack

To turn the Pre on, press and hold the power button for 2 seconds. Palm's pulsing white logo appears on the screen for as long as 90 seconds as the Pre powers up and loads the main screen (see page 15).

To turn the Pre off, press and hold the power button for 5 seconds. After that, you'll see three options on the screen; tap the one you want.

Turn Off

Airplane Mode

Cancel

- **Turn Off.** Select this option to shut down the Pre. The screen goes dark, and your incoming calls go directly to voicemail. If you're not going to use your Pre for a couple of days, choose this option to preserve battery life.

- **Airplane mode.** This option turns off all the Pre's wireless features—the phone itself, the Internet connection (see page 154), and any Bluetooth devices you paired with your Pre, like a wireless headset (see page 98). In Airplane mode, you can't communicate with the outside world, but you *can* still use the Pre's programs—to play music and games, consult your calendar, or watch a movie, for example.

> **Tip** In Airplane mode, you can manually turn on WiFi (page 41) and Bluetooth (page 41), but you can't use the phone.

- **Cancel.** Pick this option if you change your mind and want to return to the main screen. (You can also return to the main screen by pressing the center button; see page 18.)

- **Sleep/Wake.** Press the power button for just an instant to put the Pre in Sleep mode. The screen goes dark and the phone consumes very little power, but it keeps working in the background, accepting email messages, updating open web pages, and so on. The Pre wakes up when you press the power button again.

  It also wakes up when you get a phone call. The screen displays the caller's phone number (and a picture of the caller if you have his or her photo in your Contacts list—see page 214). You can either answer the call or ignore it (see Chapter 4 for the details).

Tip You can also wake the Pre by opening the keyboard (page 11).

- **Silence the ringer.** If you want to stop an incoming call from ringing, press the power button once when the call comes in.

- **Send a call to voicemail.** If you want to send an incoming call directly to voicemail, press the power button twice in quick succession.

Unlock the Pre

When you put the Pre to sleep or leave it idle for more than 30 seconds, the screen locks so that you don't accidentally press any buttons. That way, you won't run up a 45-minute phone bill by calling halfway across the world as the phone jostles around in your pocket.

Tip You can change the Pre's auto shutdown time to 1 minute, 2 minutes, or 3 minutes by going to the Launcher (see below) and tapping Screen & Lock→Screen, then tapping "Turn off after", and then choosing the interval you want.

To wake up the Pre, press the power button. A yellow circle with a lock in it at the bottom of the screen lets you know that the screen is locked. To unlock it, drag the icon from the bottom of the screen to the center of the screen.

Tip For added security, you can make your Pre ask for a PIN or password before it unlocks. Page 244 explains how to set that up.

Note If you like, you can get event notifications (see page 16) even with the Pre locked. Go to the Launcher (page 19), tap Screen & Lock→Show When Locked, and then tap On. (You still have to unlock the phone to open programs, like Email, related to any notifications.)

Ringer On/Off Switch

Slide this switch to the right to turn off the ringer and notification sounds, like the ones that play when you miss a call, get an email, or receive an instant message (page 148). This switch *doesn't* silence music, video playback, or clock alarms, however.

Tip Here's a quick way to check the ringer status: When the ringer is off, the area under the switch is red instead of black.

The ringer switch serves another purpose: move it back and forth three times while holding down the power button to reset the phone, as described on page 237.

Ringer on

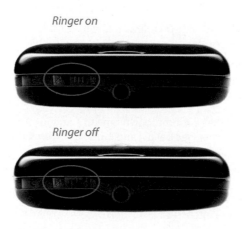

Ringer off

Note Even with the ringer off, your Pre isn't completely silent if you set it to vibrate when a call comes in (see page 85). When you get a call, you (and your neighbors) just might detect a buzzing sound. To go totally noise-free, make sure you turn off the Pre's Vibrate mode (see page 97).

Headset Jack

The Pre comes with a standard 3.5mm headphone jack, the kind found on almost every cellphone and MP3 player, so your favorite set of headphones will work fine with the Pre. But the headset that comes with the Pre has one advantage: Its cord has a built-in phone button and microphone, so you can answer a call by pressing the headset button, and talk to the caller using the headset's built-in mic.

Volume Control

The rocker button on the left side of the Pre lets you adjust the volume of the Pre's speaker, earpiece, and headphones.

Volume control

USB Connector

The right side of the Pre houses a micro-USB connector, hidden away under a plastic cover. This is where you plug in the Pre's USB cable to recharge the battery (see page 21) or to sync your Pre with your PC (see page 68).

Connector with cover removed

To get to the connector, you have to dig your fingernail underneath the plastic tab that covers it and lift the tab off. It's easier if you slide open the phone first.

The Back-Cover Latch

You'll find a single latch smack dab in the middle of the otherwise barren bottom of the Pre. Press it to remove the back cover. You have only three reasons to do this: to replace a dead battery (or to swap out a depleted battery for one that's charged), to replace the back cover if you buy the Pre's Touchstone charging accessory (see page 22), and to find your Pre's serial number.

Back cover latch

Camera and Flash

The Pre has a digital camera with a flash. With a resolution of 3 megapixels, it's a decent cellphone camera. The flash triggers automatically in low light (unless you turn that feature off). Chapter 9 has all the details.

Flash — *Camera* — *Speaker*

palm

Speaker

You'll never mistake the Pre's speaker for hi-fi audio—it's barely a step above a 1960s transistor radio. But it's good enough to serve as a ringer, work for speakerphone calls, and play sounds to remind you of appointments.

The Keyboard

Apple's iPhone has an onscreen keyboard, but many people prefer physical keys when they want to bang out emails or answer text messages. So Palm included a keyboard on the Pre, cleverly concealed behind the touchscreen.

To get to it, place your thumb on the screen, wrap your fingers around the back of the case, and gently push your thumb up so the keyboard slides out from the bottom. Chapter 2 has more about using the keyboard.

The Face of the Pre

The front of the Pre has both a touchscreen and a *gesture area*—the two primary ways you communicate with the phone—as well as a physical button. It's also where you'll find the phone's earpiece and microphone.

Earpiece

Touchscreen

Gesture area

Microphone

Center button

The Touchscreen

Your Pre's screen is touchy—but in a good way: It responds to finger taps and movements, which is how you tell the Pre what to do. So the touchscreen isn't just a display, it's also your mouse and telephone dial pad. Try it—tap the phone icon 📞 , and the dial pad pops up.

Status bar

Touchscreen

Quick Launch panel

Gesture area

The screen is divided into five sections:

- **Status bar.** This narrow strip at the top of the screen gives you info like the name of the program you're working with, the time, how much charge your battery has left, and more. It's covered in detail on the next page.

- **Touchscreen.** The touchscreen displays open programs and responds to finger taps and gestures. For more on the touchscreen, flip to page 15.

- **Quick Launch panel.** This section near the bottom of the touchscreen gives you easy access to the four most widely used applications on the Pre—the phone, your Contacts lists (page 61), the email program (page 126), and the calendar program—along with a shortcut to the Launcher (see page 19).

- **Notifications area.** You won't see this section at the bottom of the screen until you get a message letting you know about a missed call, an incoming message, a soon-to-expire battery, or some other event (see page 48 for details). When you have a lot of these alerts, the section expands and covers the Quick Launch shortcuts.

- **Gesture area.** This invisible, black, touch-sensitive area extends from the bottom of the touchscreen halfway down the center button, and spans the width of the screen. As page 18 explains, this stretch of real estate is where you perform the "back" gesture, one of the finger techniques you'll use most frequently. Chapter 2 covers all the gestures in detail.

- **Center button.** This button brings you to the Pre's Card view, explained on page 35.

Note Measured diagonally, the Pre's screen is 3.1 inches, and it has a resolution of 320 × 480 pixels. If you're into comparisons, that's the same resolution as the iPhone 3G, though the iPhone has a larger screen: 3.5 inches diagonally.

The status bar

No matter what program you use, you'll almost always see the Pre's *status bar*, an area at the top of the screen that displays a series of icons. (If you're in an application, such as when you view a web page, where turning the Pre sideways puts it into the landscape mode, the status bar goes undercover; press one of the volume keys [see page 9] to bring it back.) Here's what you see in the status bar, from left to right:

- **Application name.** The status bar's leftmost corner displays the name of the program you're currently using. Tapping the name summons the *application menu,* which lets you access features and options like cutting, copying, and pasting within that program. If you open the Photo program, for example, the word "Photo" appears here. Three exceptions: If you're using the phone, don't have any applications open, or are in Card view (see page 35), the word "Sprint" appears here instead. When you first turn on your phone or come out of Airplane mode (page 6), you'll see the word "Searching" here for a little while, as the Pre looks for a wireless signal. And if your Pre can't find a Sprint network to connect to, you'll see the words "No Service."

- **10:47. Time of day.** This one's self-explanatory: It shows the current time.

- **✳ Bluetooth.** This symbol appears when you connect your Pre to a Bluetooth device, like a wireless headset for phone calls or a "hands-free" car phone system (see page 97).

- **WiFi indicator.** As you'll learn in Chapter 7, the Pre connects to the Internet in one of three ways: through a wireless hotspot (page 155) or through one of Sprint's two cellphone networks. This icon appears when you're connected to a wireless (WiFi) hotspot. The more "sound waves" you see, the stronger the signal. WiFi is the fastest Internet connection you can have on the Pre.

- **1x or Ev R Network type.** If you're not connected to a WiFi hotspot, you'll see one of these symbols, which means you're connected to the web via one of Sprint's wireless networks. Sprint's *1x* (page 154) network is the slower of the two. With any luck, you'll be connected via Sprint's far faster network, *EvDo* (page 154). And if you see an *R* as well, you're *roaming* outside Sprint's coverage area. To surf the web, exchange email, or do any other non-phone task, you need to see one of these icons or the WiFi indicator.

> **Tip** If the Pre is transferring data, the lettering on the little icons for *1x* or *Ev* is white. If not, the lettering is black.

- **.ıll Cell signal.** This lets you know how strong your cell signal is. Don't let the fact that there are five bars fool you: If one or more are grayed out, you have a weaker signal. Ideally, you want all five bars gleaming white. If you're outside Sprint's area of coverage, the bars are not only grayed out, they also have an *X* over them.

- **✦ Airplane mode.** The plane icon tells you you're in Airplane mode (see page 6). All your wireless signals—for the phone *and* for Internet access—are off, so you won't see a WiFi or cell signal in the status bar.

- **▯ Battery meter.** If the meter is green and filled up, you've got a full charge. When the icon turns red, it's time to juice up the battery.

The touchscreen

The Pre's main display area, called the *touchscreen*, is where the action is most of the time. It's the Pre's equivalent of a PC's desktop—it displays open programs and serves as the conduit for communications between you and the Pre. It's one of the two places that responds to the finger gestures that tell the Pre what to do (the other is the gesture area; see page 18).

If you have a program open, the touchscreen displays a miniature screen shot of the program, which Palm calls an *activity card*. If you have several programs open, the touchscreen displays a set of cards, one beside the other, as in the image below. Palm calls this overview look at open programs the *Card view*. To work within one of the programs, tap its card. The application takes over the touchscreen and you're ready to get to work.

Quick Launch panel

As mentioned on page 13, the Quick Launch panel gives you shortcuts to the programs you use most often. Think of it as Palm's version of the Windows Toolbar or the Mac OS X's Dock.

The panel has five shortcuts: for the phone 📞, your Contacts list 📇 (see page 61), the email program ✉ (see page 126), and the calendar program 📅 (see page 105) in that order. The fifth link takes you to the Launcher ⊙ , a master list of all the programs installed on your Pre (including the Quick Launch panel and its icons). You can remove or replace any of the Quick Launch panel icons (see page 33) except the one for the Launcher, because you'll always need a way to get to the Launcher.

Notifications area

The Pre lets you know when you receive or miss a call, get an email, get a program update, and on several other occasions.

Notifications, discussed in detail on page 48, give you just enough informa-tion to clue you in on whether you have to drop what you're doing and act on something immediately. They typically combine a line or two of text with an icon; sometimes, though, they're just tiny icons. For example, a notification may let you know that you have an email with the subject "Urgent, Please Reply," or that you missed a call from your boss.

After a few seconds, most alerts you ignore shrink down to icons in the bottom-right corner of the notifications area (see page 48). Tap one of those icons to get more info.

Minimized notifications for a phone call
and a calendar appointment

Gesture area

As you learned earlier, the Pre interprets finger movements, which Palm calls *gestures*, as commands. You perform these gestures in two places—on the touchscreen and in what Palm calls the *gesture area*, a region just below the main display.

While you can use gestures in both these areas, some are interpreted differently depending on where you do them. For instance, swiping your finger from right to left in the gesture area issues the Back command. Doing the same thing on the touchscreen advances you from one application to the next. See page 26 in Chapter 2 and page 239 in Appendix C for more about the gesture area.

The Center Button

Pressing the lone button on the front of the Pre (shown on page 12) changes what you see on the touchscreen. If you're working within an application, for example, pressing the center button brings you back to *Card view*. If you're in Card view and you press the center button, the center card becomes your working program and takes over the screen.

The Launcher

As mentioned above, the Pre provides links to every program on your phone in a program library Palm calls the Launcher. You get to the Launcher by pressing its icon ⬤, which is the only permanent member of the Quick Launch panel. To open an application in the Launcher, tap its icon.

Many of the Pre's programs—its web browser, its MP3 player, and its camera, for example—are discussed in depth later in the book. But other, smaller programs and settings you find here deserve special mention:

- **Clock.** You can choose whether you want to see a digital or analog-style clock and set an alarm. A little alarm notification at the bottom of the touchscreen reminds you when you've set an alarm. (You can select this notification and swipe it off the screen—page 49 tells you how to do that—and the alarm will still go off.)

- **Calculator.** Need to figure out a meal tip? Help Junior with his homework? This application lets you do simple arithmetic. Press the space bar to summon the square root and percentage keys that aren't shown when you first open the calculator.

- **Doc View and PDF View.** These applications let you look at Microsoft Office files (Doc View) and Adobe PDF files (PDF View) that arrive attached to email messages or that you add to your Pre through a USB connection (see page 184). As of this writing, you can't edit these documents, but DataViz, a software company that works closely with Palm, is developing a program to let you do so.

- **Date & Time.** Choose between a 12- or 24-hour time format. You can also have the Pre automatically set your time zone clock by turning "Network time zone" on. Or turn "Network time zone" off and manually choose a time zone from a list of cities and countries around the world. The latter option can come in handy if you're traveling but want to stay on your home body-clock, or if you're staying put but want to be simpatico with clients in Asia.

- **Device Info.** Tap this icon to see a raft of info about the Pre itself: how much memory the device has and how much is free, the amount of battery life left, your phone number, and so on. You can also find the Pre's serial number here. If you ever have a problem with your Pre, someone in Palm's support department may ask you to open this screen.

- **Updates.** Sprint occasionally updates the Pre's operating system, webOS (see page 49), to fix problems or add features. Sprint notifies you when an update comes out, but if you're a Type A personality, you can check for them manually here. If there are updates to the programs you downloaded through the App Catalog (see page 225), you can fetch those here, too.

- **Backup.** Once you set up a Palm Profile (see page 3), Palm automatically backs up all the information on your Pre each day. You can request an immediate backup here by tapping "Back up now."

- **Language.** You can operate your Pre in either English or Español.

- **Sprint.** This is a shortcut to Sprint's website, where you can see a list of frequently asked questions about the Pre or view instructional videos.

- **App Catalog.** Though it is still in beta (test) mode at the time of this writing, Palm's App Catalog (see Appendix B) is the place to sample, rate, buy, and download third-party programs. (They're called *third-party programs* because they're created by companies and individuals other than Palm.) Among the dozen or so applications available when the Pre debuted: Pandora Internet radio, Fandango movie show times, *The New York Times*, and Classic, which makes your Pre act like one of Palm's earlier devices, such as the Treo or Palm Pilot. New applications are being added all the time. Click this icon to see what's out there.

The Prescient Pre

Your Pre knows which way you're holding it (vertically or horizontally, up to your ear or down at your side) and puts that knowledge to good use. Three high-tech sensors tell the Pre which way is up:

- **Proximity sensor.** When you bring the phone up to your ear during a phone call, the Pre darkens the display to save power and keep your cheek cool. (It doesn't do this when you use the speakerphone, however.) It also disables the touchscreen to prevent any inadvertent button-tapping.

- **Accelerometer.** When you turn the Pre from vertical to horizontal, the screen orientation changes from portrait to landscape mode. Try it with web pages and pictures.

- **Light sensor.** If you're in a dimly lit room, the Pre dims the display to save battery power.

The Battery

Your Pre's battery comes partially charged, but eventually you'll have to juice it up yourself. And you may have to replace a battery, either to swap it with a fully charged spare or when the original battery no longer holds a charge. This section tells you how.

Recharge the Battery

You recharge the Pre's battery two ways:

- **AC adapter.** Plug the small end of the Pre's USB cable into the phone's micro-USB connector (see page 9) and the other end into the AC adapter. Then plug the adapter into a wall socket. The Pre briefly displays a "Charging Battery" message in the notification area to let you know it's powering up. A full charge takes up to two and a half hours, Palm says.

Tip If you unscrew the top of the AC adapter, you can switch from a plug that works in North America to one that works in Europe, Australia, and Argentina, though you'll also have to buy an international power charger. You can get one from Palm for about $40 at *http://tinyurl.com/n92ubn*.

- **USB cable.** Connect the small end of the cable into the Pre's micro-USB connector, and plug the large end into a standard USB slot on your PC. It takes longer to charge the Pre this way, about 4½ hours. If your phone is off when you recharge it via the USB cable, the Pre doesn't display a charging message.

Buyers' Guide

A High-Tech Recharge

Another way to juice up your battery is with Palm's Touchstone Charging Kit, which costs $70 from Palm (though you might find it for less online). The Touchstone charges the Pre when you place the phone on top of the dock—it generates an electromagnetic field via a set of internal coils, and magnets hold the phone in place. You replace the Pre's stock back cover with an "inductive" one that transmits the charge. From then on, you don't have to fiddle with AC adapters or USB cables (though you do have to plug in the Touchstone, of course).

The Pre gets charged at the same rate as if you'd plugged it into the wall, and the dock tilts the screen toward you so you can see notification messages.

The Touchstone has a few other tricks: If your Pre is lying on the dock when a call comes in, the phone automatically answers when you pick it up. And if you're on a call and place the Pre on the dock, the speakerphone automatically comes on. When lying on the Touchstone, the Pre displays a clock with a digital readout.

Replace the Battery

Unlike the iPhone, the Pre has a battery you can swap out or replace. But getting at it is a slightly tricky maneuver that involves pressing and letting go of the back-cover release (see page 10), and then sliding your thumbnail between the cover and the phone as you lift the cover up by its sides. To remove the old battery, lift it out by grabbing the tab at the top. Then insert the new battery, and snap the cover back on.

> **Tip** When pushing the back-cover release to lift the cover off, stick a fingernail in just under the cover to pop the bottom open and then run your fingernail along the sides to completely dislodge it. You can also try sticking a credit card between the back cover and the phone to yank it off.

If you use your Pre constantly, you may want to buy a spare battery (about $50) so you can always have a fully charged one on hand. The Appendix on page 234 has tips for preserving battery life.

Chapter
2

Move Around the Pre

Aside from making calls (and sometimes even then), cellphones can be so complex that that they'd stymie a CIA code-breaker. Going from an address book to a Missed Calls screen, for example, can involve labyrinthine menus and confusing "soft" keys.

On the other hand, *smartphones*—mobile phones that you can use to check your email and browse the web—typically hamstring you in other ways, like limiting you to one task at a time. You can send an email, but not while listening to music. Or you can surf the web, but you can't check your calendar, too. As a result, you usually end up opening and closing programs all day long. That's not the way your desktop PC works, and it shouldn't be the way your smartphone works, either.

Fortunately, the Pre sets things right: It simplifies menu navigation with a library of easy-to-use gestures, lets you open multiple applications at once, and lets you switch among them easily and logically.

In this chapter, you'll learn how to control the Pre using gestures, how to switch from one program to another, and how to take advantage of some special characteristics of the Pre's keyboard.

Finger Tips: Six Ways to Navigate the Pre

You interact with the Pre through a variety of *gestures,* finger motions that the Pre recognizes as commands. The six techniques described below will have you finger-tapping your way through the Pre in no time. But first, you need to know where to make these gestures.

Touchscreen vs. Gesture Area

As you'll see in this chapter, you have to do some finger gestures on the touchscrean, some in the gesture area below the touchscreen, and some you can do across both areas. In other words, *where* you perform gestures matters, too.

Gestures in the gesture area do things similar to what physical buttons on traditional cellphones do. For example, when you do the right-to-left swipe or back gesture (see next page) in the gesture area, it takes you up one level in the hierarchy of screens. On a conventional cellphone, you'd probably use a Back button to do this.

On the other hand, when you swipe in either direction on the touchscreen with, for example, the Photos application open (page 210), you go back and forth from one picture to the next.

Tap

Fred Astaire never tapped as often as you will on the Pre. You tap the touchscreen to open an application, select menu options, and position the cursor.

To tap, touch the screen with your fingertip using a fast and firm motion. The Pre confirms your tap by displaying a white ripple where you touched the screen.

Swipe

To perform a swipe, move your finger across the screen in one quick, smooth, constant motion, and then lift your finger just as quickly. Swiping serves a couple of purposes on the Pre, depending on whether you swipe in the gesture area or on the main touchscreen, and on whether you move left to right or right to left. Below are some examples of each type of swipe.

The right-to-left swipe

This motion, commonly known as the *back swipe,* is the star of the swipe team. You use it often in the gesture area, and here's why: As you go deeper into a program, this motion lets you retrace your steps screen by screen, so you can back up one level at a time until you return to your starting point, the program's opening screen.

For example, say you want to listen to the song "Speed of Sound," by the band Coldplay. You go to Music Library→Artists→Coldplay→Speed of Sound (page 192 has more about the music library). Then you decide you'd rather hear "Viva La Vida." Back swipe in the gesture area to go up one level to Coldplay's songs list, and then tap "Viva La Vida." If you then decide to listen to Pink instead, back-swipe twice to go up two levels to Artists, and then tap "Pink."

The back swipe serves a couple of other purposes:

- If there's no previous screen when you back swipe within an application, you return to Card view (see page 36).

- If you're watching a video, it moves the video back 10 seconds.

> **Tip** In most cases, when you move back from one screen to another using the back swipe, the Pre automatically saves what you were working on. For instance, if you're writing a memo and perform the back gesture to get back to a list of all your memos, the Pre saves the memo you were composing. (If you see a Done button after a back swipe, you have to tap Done to save your work.)

The left-to-right swipe

The Pre rarely uses this gesture. You use this kind of swipe to move a video ahead. How far ahead depends on the length of the video: 30 seconds for videos longer than a minute, 10 seconds for all others.

Drag

This gesture—where you slowly move your finger across the touchscreen without lifting it—lets you:

- Move within a page that's too large for the Pre's display area. For example, you can drag your finger in any direction (including diagonally) to move a web page or map around so you can focus on a particular area.

- Scroll through a list line by line; simply lift your finger when you see the menu item or name you're looking for.

- Reposition cards and program icons (see page 38).

- Close programs (see page 39).

- Delete items from lists.

Dragging is great for things you want to do slowly and carefully. But it's *too* slow when you want to do something quickly, like zip through a list of 200 song titles. In cases like that, flicking is the gesture you want.

Flick

Flicking is the primo way to scroll through *long* lists, like a set of contacts or your music library. To perform this gesture, you do just what you'd expect: Put your finger on the Pre's touchscreen, move your finger really quickly either up or down or left or right, and then lift it.

Once you flick a list, it starts out scrolling fast, then slows down, and, after a few seconds, finally stops. The faster you flick, the farther up or down (or right or left) in a list you go. If you skitter past the point where you want to stop, tap the screen to stop the scroll, and drag the list back to the name or list item you want.

Pinch-and-Spread

Sometimes you want to zoom in on an area of a screen—to make it easier to read the content on a web page, for example, or to enlarge a map or photo. That's where this gesture comes in: Put your thumb and forefinger together, place them on the touchscreen, and then spread them apart (this is called *pinching out*).

The downside to zooming in is that you can't see a whole page. To regain your bearings, zoom out by *pinching in,* bringing your separated thumb and forefinger together on the touchscreen.

Double-Tap

Pinching isn't the only way to zoom. Double-tap an area of the touchscreen, such as a column of a news story on the web, and the Pre enlarges the area you touched. Double-tap a second time to zoom back out. Double-tap zooming works for web pages, photos, and documents.

Tip If you're having trouble getting the Pre to respond to your gestures, see page 239 in Appendix C for some possible fixes.

The Program-to-Program Shortcut

- If you have an application open and you want to switch to another open program, you normally have to jump to Card view first (see page 38). But there is a way to go from program to program without stopping at Card view along the way. To do so, you use a gesture that's similar to the swipes you learned on page 27. Before you can use it, though, you have to change one of the Pre's settings:

- From the third page of the Launcher (page 33 explains how to get there), tap Screen & Lock→Advanced Gestures. Tap the button beside Switch Applications to move it from Off to On.

- Now that your settings are correct, you can use this spiffy shortcut: When you're in an application and you do a full swipe in the gesture area (move your finger left to right across the entire gesture area), your Pre opens the last application you were working in, instead of going to the previous screen of your current application (as it would if you hadn't turned on the Switch Applications setting). Swipe the other way, from right to left, and you go to the next application in line.

- The order of the applications depends on the order you opened them in Card view. For example, say you open application A, then application B, and finally application C. Then you start working in application B. With Switch Applications on, a left-to-right swipe takes you to application A, and a right-to-left swipe (aka a back swipe) takes you to application C.

- Does this mean you can't use a back swipe to switch to a previous screen anymore? No, but you have to modify that gesture slightly: Your back swipes need to be much shorter and more controlled than full swipes, spanning no more than halfway across the gesture area.

Working with Programs

One of the Pre's big advantages is that it can *multitask*—have several programs open and active at once. In this section, you'll learn how to open programs, move among them, and work within them.

The Pre gives you three ways to open programs: The first two are through the Quick Launch panel and the Launcher. You'll learn about the third way, using the Pre's universal search feature, a little later in this chapter.

Quick Launch Panel

As you learned in the last chapter, Palm figures you'll use certain programs all the time, so they've put shortcuts for those programs—Phone, Email, Contacts, and Calendar—in the *Quick Launch panel.* Tap one of the program's icons to open that program.

The Quick Launch panel is always at the bottom of the Pre's touchscreen (see page 12) when you're in Card view (page 36). But you're not always in Card view. For example, if you're working in an application, you don't see the Quick Launch panel. In cases like that, you can pull up a "floating" version of the panel, which looks like something out of the psychedelic '60s.

Here's how to do that: Drag your finger from the gesture area toward the center of the touchscreen. As you cross the border between the two, a bendy version of the Quick Launch panel pops up, looking a bit like a shape-shifting boomerang. Keep your finger on the panel, and slide it over to the program you want to open. The Pre displays the application's name to confirm your choice. Simply lift your finger to open that application.

Customize Quick Launch

If *your* list of most-used programs differs from Palm's, you can replace any of the first four shortcuts in the Quick Launch panel with one of your choosing (you can't replace the fifth icon, which opens the Launcher).

First, you need to free up space in the panel: In the Quick Launch panel, tap and hold the icon you want to replace until a blue halo appears around it, and then drag it onto the Launcher icon and let it go. Next, go into the Launcher and tap and hold the icon you want to add to Quick Launch, and then drag *that* icon to the Quick Launch panel's now-vacant slot and let go.

> **Note** You don't *need* to have five icons in the Quick Launch panel. If you want, you can remove all the icons from the panel except the Launcher's. But you might as well use the panel for the applications you cherish the most.

The Launcher

While the Quick Launch panel is a handy way to open often-used programs, it can't show you all the programs on your Pre. To see the complete list, you need to go to Quick Launch's big brother, the Launcher, which you can think of as the Pre's version of the "home" screen you find on other smartphones.

Open the Launcher in one of these ways:

- In Card view (see page 36), tap the Quick Launch panel's Launcher icon.

- In Card view, flick from the gesture area toward the touchscreen.

- In any other view, press the center button (see page 18) to switch to Card view, and then tap the Quick Launch panel's Launcher icon.

- From within an application, flick twice from the gesture area toward the touchscreen. (This takes practice; you may inadvertently drag up the Quick Launch panel until you get the hang of it.)

With the Launcher open, you'll see icons for all the programs on your Pre. Launcher icons behave just like the ones in the Quick Launch panel—simply tap one to open a program. To reposition a Launcher icon, tap and hold it until you see a blue halo around it, and then drag the icon to the new spot and release it.

The Launcher is actually made up of three screens. On the first Launcher screen, you see two short, vertical white bars at the bottom-right edge of the screen, which lets you know that there are two other screens. If you flip to the second screen by swiping from right to left, one of these white bars appears on the screen's bottom right, and another at the bottom left, to let you know you can move either forward or back to another screen. And if you're on the third Launcher screen, both markers are at the bottom left.

Page markers

Frequently used programs like Web (see page 160), Camera (see page 203), and Photos (see page 207) programs appear on the first Launcher screen. On the second screen, you'll find entertainment applications like Sprint TV (see page 199), Amazon MP3 (see page 185), and YouTube (see page 197). Settings like Sounds & Ringtones (see page 93), Wi-Fi (which this book will refer to as WiFi; see page 157), and Bluetooth (see page 97) are on the third. Palm says it considered how often applications are likely to be used in determining the order of the icons. If you like, you can change what appears on each screen by dragging icons off one screen and parking them on another.

Out of the box, your Pre already has more applications than the Launcher can display on its three screens, so you may have to scroll up or down a screen to find the program you're looking for. Tiny arrows at the top and bottom of the Launcher screen indicate whether there are icons above or below what's showing on a screen. For example, if you're at the top of a long screen, you see a tiny arrow at the bottom to let you know that you can scroll down to find more icons. A faster way to find applications you add—page 225 explains how to add programs—is the universal search feature you'll learn about on page 47.

To close the Launcher, place your finger in the middle of the touchscreen and flick straight down into the gesture area. (Flick back up to open it again.) Do the same thing when you're in Card view, and the center card becomes the active application.

The Concept of Cards

When you open multiple programs, you need a way to see them all at once and to switch from one to another. In Windows, you do that with the taskbar, and on the Mac, you use the Dock, but those setups won't work on the Pre's small screen. So Palm came up with a new metaphor: a set of cards. The Pre represents each of your open applications with an *activity card*, a miniature picture of the application. If you have five programs open, five activity cards are laid out side by side across the middle of the screen. This is called *Card view,* which you'll learn more about in a second. Depending on the size of the cards and how many there are, you may not be able to see them all at once. (And if you have no programs open, you won't see any cards.)

Even though they're tiny, these cards are exact representations of the programs they stand for. So, for example, if you have the Web application (see page 160) open, the web page shown on the Web card gets updated if the info on that page changes. You can drag (see page 28) or flick (see page 29) these cards to move between the applications. To start working with a program, tap its card. That application takes over the screen, and from that point on, you're working in that program.

Card View: Your Programs at a Glance

The best way to understand Card view is to try it out. Go to the Quick Launch panel, tap the Launcher icon, and then tap the icon labeled "Memos." The Memos program opens full-screen, and you're working within that application. To switch to Card view, use the back swipe gesture you learned earlier (see page 27): From the Memos main screen, swipe from right to left in the gesture area. The Pre shrinks the Memos program down to an activity card and takes you to Card view.

In the image above, you only see one card, for the Memos program, because that's the only application you have open. To make things a little more interesting, go to the Quick Launch panel at the bottom of Card view and tap the phone icon.

The Pre opens the Phone program and fills the display with the application's opening screen (the dial pad). To get back to Card view, back swipe in the gesture area just as you did before. Now you see two cards: One for Memos and one for Phone. The card representing the program you just came from (in this case, Phone) always appears in the center of the Card view. If you want to switch to Memos again, drag the cards to the right until the Memos card is centered, and then tap it.

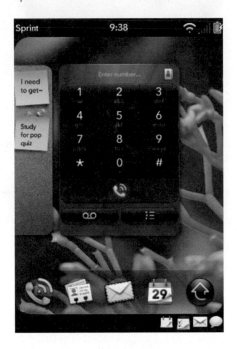

Note There's a limit to how many cards you can have open simultaneously, but it's not a hard-and-fast number: It's based on memory use, so you may be able to keep 10 or more cards open at once. When you bump up against the limit, you'll get a not-so-subtle onscreen message saying that, before you can open a new card, you to have discard another.

As you learned in this example, you can use the back-swipe gesture to go to Card view. But Card view is so important—it's your hub for switching from one program to another—that the Pre gives you several ways to get there. Perhaps the most prominent is the center button.

The center button

The *center button* is a fail-safe way to get to Card view, no matter where you are on the Pre. It's the only physical button on the front of the Pre.

When you press the center button while you're in a program, the program shrinks down and becomes the center card in Card view, and it's flanked by cards for any other programs you have open.

> **Note** Little hidden lights sit on either side of the center button, and there's one in the center button itself. These light up when you perform gestures in the gesture area. Oddly, the center button *doesn't* light up when you press it to go into Card view.

Other paths to Card view

You can reach Card view in a couple of other ways. From within an application, do one of the following:

- Flick from the gesture area to the center of the touchscreen.

- From within an application, keep doing the back-swipe gesture until you've reached the last possible screen in the program. One more back swipe takes you to
Card view.

Rearranging cards

You can change the order of cards in Card view if, for example, you want to keep all your open web pages grouped together, or if you want to group your email messages.

To reorder cards, simply drag and drop them: Tap and hold a card until it shrinks and becomes transparent; when you do, all the other cards shrink to an even smaller degree. (Alternatively, you can tap near—but not on—a card to make them all shrink at once.) Then drag the transparent card to a new spot and lift your finger.

How to Open Programs in Card View

You can open an application in Card view five ways:

- Tap the card for the application you want to open.

- If the card for the application is in the center of the screen, press the center button.

- Drag cards until you center the application you want, and then press the center button.

- Flick the application's card down from the touchscreen to the gesture area.

- Start typing the application's name, which automatically invokes universal search until its name and icon appear. (see page 46), and then tap the icon.

Close Programs and Delete Files

Closing a program on the Pre is rewarding because it gives you the same sense of satisfaction as a good housecleaning. When you finish with a program—you're done listening to music, say, or reviewing photos—go to Card view, and then drag or flick the card off the top of the screen. (Yes, you always have to go to Card view to close a program, but you quickly get the hang of it.)

The Pre automatically closes the application. But don't worry: This has no effect on the program's *files,* so your songs, web history, photos, and the like are still on your Pre.

If you *do* want to delete something—a file like an email message or text message, or a list item like an entry on your Tasks list (see page 119)—drag the file or list item horizontally off the screen to either side. The Pre may ask for confirmation, in which case you tap Delete, and the item walks the plank.

> **Tip** If you want to get rid of several items in a single window and there's a Delete prompt, keep dragging over the items until you're done, and only then tap Delete. You don't have to tap Delete for each item individually.

The Corner Menus

As you learned in Chapter 1 (see page 14), you'll find two menus in the Pre's status bar, one at the left end of the bar, and one at the right end. The left menu, called the *application menu*, is for program options, and the right one is for the Pre's networks and other info like the date and battery status. This section explains these two menus in detail.

Application menus

When you work in an application, the Pre displays the name of the program in an oval at the left end of the status bar. Tap anywhere in the oval (it takes a little practice to hit the right spot) to open the program's application menu.

What you see in this menu depends on what application you're using. The menu that comes up when you have your web browser open, for example, includes selections for Bookmarks and History; if you have your calendar open, you see menu items that let you jump to a specific date. Almost all application menus have a Preferences option, so you can fine-tune the way each program works. (You'll learn more about these settings in the sections of this book dedicated to each program.)

If a menu item is grayed out, it means you can't select that option. If a menu item has a right-pointing arrow, there are options within that command; tap the arrow to see them. A downward-pointing arrow at the bottom of a menu means that the program offers even more options; tap the arrow to see them.

Some applications have ad hoc menus in addition to the standard upper-corner menus. For example, if you tap the Menu button in Google Maps, you can search a map, see traffic patterns, get directions, overlay a satellite view of the map, and more.

Network menu

Tap the upper-right corner of the status bar (where the signal-strength bar is) to turn your WiFi and Bluetooth network connections on or off, and to set preferences for each. (Chapter 4 and Chapter 7 tell you all about these networks.) The menu also displays the current date, how much battery life you have left, and an on/off switch for Airplane mode (see page 6).

Working with the Keyboard

You can do an awful lot on the Pre with finger gestures alone, but the keyboard has a few features of its own. You use it to thumb-type web addresses and email messages, for example, and to use the Pre's powerful universal search feature (page 46). This section explains all the things you can do with the keyboard.

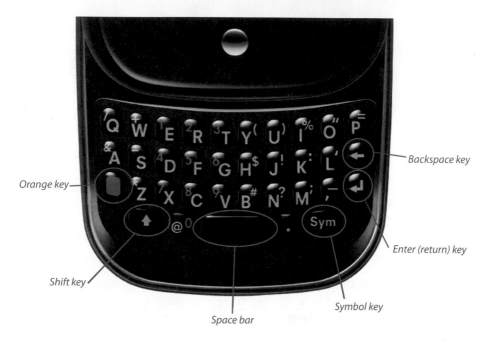

Backspace key

Orange key

Enter (return) key

Shift key

Symbol key

Space bar

The Orange Key

At some point, you'll need to put parentheses in an email, or a dollar sign in a text message. These special characters appear above the alphabetic keys on the keyboard. To type them, press and release the orange key, and then press the corresponding letter key. You'll know you're in special-character mode when the Pre displays a blue circle just below the blinking cursor. Unless you press the orange key again, the Pre automatically switches back to regular mode after you type in a single special character. To lock in the keys for the special set of characters—so you can type several of them in a row—press the orange key twice; a black circle confirms your choice. Press the orange key again to return to the standard keyboard mode.

Single-key special characters

Special character set locked in

The orange key can do a few other tricks. Press orange key+Sym+R to perform a "soft" reset of the Pre (see page 236). Hold down the orange key when you tap a Launcher icon to display the version number for that application and, unless it's a program that came on your Pre from the factory, to delete that program.

The Symbol Key

The Pre's symbol key, marked "Sym" on the keyboard (see page 11), opens a whole new world of characters, including numerical fractions (like ½), trademark symbols (™), and smiley faces—☺,☹. Press Sym to open a table of all the available symbols, then drag your finger to scroll through the table until you find the character you want. Tap it to add it to your document.

The Sym button is your gateway to variations on standard letters, too. If you need an acute accent to say you're trés impressed with your new Pre, for example, press Sym and then the appropriate letter key to narrow down the table of symbols to ones associated with that letter—in this case, *E*.

Position the Cursor

As you write emails or add contacts to your address book, you'll have to correct errors, add text, or otherwise edit your entries. To do that, you need a way to position the Pre's cursor. On most phones, you tap in the general vicinity of the text you want to edit and then use arrow keys to precisely position the cursor. Alas, the Pre's keyboard, handy though it is, lacks arrow keys (save for a destructive back-arrow key that eliminates either the character you just typed or—if you press the Shift key ♠ simultaneously—the entire last word).

Here's how you position the cursor: Tap the screen as close to where you want it to go as possible. If you get it just right, congratulations! If not, then hold down the keyboard's orange key, and drag the cursor to the precise edit point.

> **Tip** Dragging the cursor while pressing the orange key requires a steady hand. If you're not paying attention, you might accidentally press the adjacent * key and type an asterisk. Fortunately, you don't have to hold your finger precisely on the onscreen cursor—you can put your finger above or below the cursor so you can see the text as you find a new insertion point.

Cut, Copy, and Paste

The Pre lets you cut, copy, and paste text, but first you need to select the text. Position the cursor as described above, and then press and hold the Shift key ⬆ while you drag the cursor across the text. The Pre highlights your selection in yellow.

Next, tap the upper-left corner of the screen to display the application menu, and then tap Edit→Cut or Edit→Copy. Next, position the cursor, and then open the application menu and tap Edit→Paste. If you want to paste that text into a different program, open the destination application, position your cursor, and then go to the application menu and tap Edit→Paste.

You can also use keyboard shortcuts to edit text. After you highlight the text and position the cursor where you want to edit the text, tap and hold the gesture area—you see the center button light up—and then press X to cut, C to copy, or V to paste the text.

> **Note** Cut, copy, and paste only work on *editable* text, like that in email messages or memos. You can't copy text from a web page, for example (but you *can* share a picture of a web page in an email, as discussed on page 164).

Search the Pre (and Beyond)

One of the Pre's coolest features is *universal search*. As you type in a search term, universal search goes through *every* contact name and application on your Pre looking for a match.

To use universal search, you have to be in Card view (page 36) or in the Launcher (page 33). From either spot, simply start typing on the keyboard. The moment you strike a key, the Pre figures you want to send out a search party. It immediately finds all the contacts and application names that match what you've typed so far. As you continue to type, it narrows down its suggestions. So if you type in *gre,* the search results might include first names like Greg, last names like Greene, and applications like Greektranslations (if there were such a Pre application). If you continue to type, say, *en,* only Greene remains in the list. If that's who you're looking for, tap the name to open Sally Greene's profile in the Pre's Contacts program (see page 61), where you can tap her phone number to call her, tap her email address to drop her a note, and so on.

> **Tip** Universal search automatically highlights in blue the first item in its list of suggestions. If you want to select the second item in that list or any item below that, just tap it.

But universal search gets even better. The moment you type a character that eliminates matches on the Pre, the phone expands your search to the web: It replaces the search results list with tabs for Google, Google Maps, Wikipedia, and Twitter. So if you want to search the web for info about Wisconsin's football team, type *Green Bay Packers* and then tap Google or Wikipedia.

You can use universal search to find phone numbers, too, and as a shortcut for opening applications. For example, if you type *g,* a Google Maps shortcut appears; tap it to open the program. Tap M for shortcuts to Memos, Music, Messaging, Amazon MP3 and—yet again—Google Maps.

Universal search isn't perfect, though. It could do a much better job of searching *within* applications on the Pre. As of this writing, it doesn't search emails, multimedia messages, memos, tasks, photos, videos, music files, or Word, Excel, PowerPoint, or PDF files.

Notifications and Updates

The Pre reserves a small strip of screen real estate at the bottom edge of the touchscreen to flag important events, such as incoming or missed calls, voice-mails, email and text messages, low battery warnings, and so on. Palm calls it the *notification area*, and its size changes depending on how many notifications you have; if you don't have any, the notifications area is hidden.

Notifications pop up as you work, without interrupting what you're doing. They initially appear as tiny icons with a few words of text. To respond to one, tap it, and the Pre opens the appropriate program. For example, if you tap an email message notification, the Pre transports you to the Email application and opens the new message. (Don't worry—tapping a notification won't close whatever else you're working on.)

> **Tip** Notifications are meant to be unobtrusive, but you may be put off by the bell clang that accompanies them. If so, go to Launcher→Sounds & Ringtones→System Sounds, and set the volume slider to an appropriate level. You can also silence the bell completely by turning the System Sounds setting from On to Off, or by sliding the ringer switch on top of the Pre to its off position (see page 6).

If you're busy and don't respond to a notification right away, it morphs into a mini-icon in the lower-right portion of the screen, which is still technically part of the notification area. If you set an alarm (see page 19), the alarm notification begins life as a bell-shaped icon in that lower-right corner. At the appointed time, the alarm notification takes over the bottom of the screen—you have the option to dismiss it or to tap Snooze to get a 5-minute respite. Some notifications, like the one for "Charging Battery", are just FYI—you don't need to do anything.

Tap on one of these mini-icons to make that notification reappear in what's called the *notifications dashboard*. This dashboard grabs part of the touchscreen from whatever application you're working on, or, if you're in Card view, it covers up the Quick Launch panel.

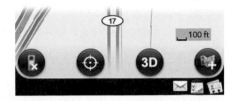

If you have several notifications in the notification dashboard, they get stacked on top of each other. If one notification is more important than another, you can reorder the stack by tapping, holding, and dragging a notification to a new spot. To delete a notification, simply drag it off the side of the screen.

System Updates

From time to time, Palm improves the Pre's operating system, webOS (see page 5). If Palm notifies you of a system upgrade, you can install it immediately (by tapping Install Now) or whenever you want (by tapping Install Later).

Well, *almost* whenever: If you don't install system updates right away, the Pre keeps after you until you do. You can put it off a total of three times, but after that the Pre takes over. Your only choice in the fourth prompt is Install Now. And Palm's not fooling around—if your battery's at least 30 percent charged, the Pre installs the update. If not, it'll wait until the Pre gets some juice.

> **Note** If you have your WiFi network turned on (see page 155) and your battery is at least 30 percent charged, the Pre automatically *downloads* system updates without prompting you, though it still prompts you before installing them.
>
> If you have WiFi turned off, Palm checks your Pre for two days, and then tries to send you the file via Sprint's EvDo network (see page 154), as long as you have at least 30 percent battery life left. But Palm won't attempt the download if you have a pokier Sprint network connection or if your battery slips under the 30 percent threshold. Palm and Sprint also consider your pocketbook: They won't download the update if you're roaming, which could cost you a bundle.

If you take the plunge and install upgrades as they come out, the process is pretty painless: You can continue working while the update downloads, but you have to stop while the Pre actually installs the upgrade. Afterward, the Pre automatically resets your phone. Tap Done, and you are.

Application Updates

You'll eventually buy and install programs from companies other than Palm through the App Catalog (see page 225). And, just like Palm, these companies update their programs. If you get an application update notice, tap the notification icon, and your Pre opens the App Catalog and takes you to a page with info about that update—why the publisher is issuing it, for example, and what program flaws the update corrects.

> **Tip** You can manually check for application updates by tapping Updates in the Launcher. You can also check the App Catalog for updates to your programs. If there is one, the programs display a blue arrow over their icon.

Some updates are free, while others will cost you. If a company issues a program update to fix a bug, for example, the download is usually free. But if the company introduces something like a new feature, you might have to pay for the upgrade. (Of course, you can decline the update and continue working with the "old" program.)

You can install the free updates independently of the for-pay versions. In the App Catalog, tap Install Free to fetch the gratis updates only, or tap Install All to download every update, both free and for-pay.

As with system updates, you can use the phone while the Pre downloads the updates, but not while it installs them. But program updates don't usually take long.

Chapter

3

Sync the Pre

Your Pre is almost always with you, but the information you care about is scattered all over the place--on your Facebook page, in web-based email programs like Gmail, on your PC at work, and on your laptop at home. In an ideal world, you'd be able to tap into this scattered information anywhere, anytime. That's the goal behind a program on your Pre called Palm Synergy, which is part of webOS (see page 5). Synergy keeps the information on your Pre and in your online accounts in sync with each other.

In this chapter, you'll learn how to use Synergy to collect and catalogue information from your online accounts to your Pre, how to sync information on your Pre back to those accounts, and how to jerry-rig a system to keep even your desktop and laptop PCs synced with the Pre.

Synergy Close-Up

During a sync, Synergy imports and exports information to and from your Pre. On the import side of the sync, Synergy gathers, organizes, and (within limits) saves to your Pre the data in your online accounts. That way, you always have a single, consolidated set of email messages, friends' addresses, calendar events, and so on, in your pocket.

In addition to this consolidated view, the Pre lets you view information by source, so you can, for example, change your calendar display from the consolidated view to one that shows events from your Google calendar only.

The export side of the sync is a little more complex. You can add new information to three types of account: to a linked online account that you specify (such as a Google or Microsoft Exchange account), to the Pre only (a.k.a. your Palm Profile account), or to an account that you designate as a *default account*, explained below.

Here's how that works: Say you're viewing events you scheduled in your Google calendar by selecting the Google calendar view in the Pre's Calendar program. If you add an event while in this view, Synergy adds the event to your online Google calendar the next time it syncs. (After that sync, the event shows up in your consolidated calendar view, too, of course, because the Pre collects and aggregates your online information.)

If you want to add an event to the Pre's calendar only, you select the Palm Profile calendar view (because the Palm Profile calendar is really just another name for the Pre calendar), and the event you schedule stays on your Pre; it doesn't get synced anywhere online.

Finally, if you're in the consolidated calendar view and you add an event there, Synergy needs to know which calendar it should add the event to. You don't want it to do so across all your accounts—the reason you have separate accounts, after all, is to keep your information in different, logical places—you want your work and personal calendars as separate entities, for example. That's the idea behind the default account. When you don't specify an account as a destination for information you add to the Pre, Synergy uses your default account. So if, in the example above, you add an event in the consolidated calendar view, that event gets added to whatever account you designated as your default. (You'll learn more about your default account a little later in this chapter.)

What Synergy Imports

Think of Synergy as an information coordinator. It collects information from the online accounts listed below and displays it all in a single view on your Pre. So if you keep your friends' profile information (phone numbers, email addresses, and so on) in a Google address book and your coworkers' profiles on Facebook, Synergy collects both sets of contact info, combines them with each other and with any contacts you've added to the Pre, and consolidates everything into a single contacts list.

> **Note** For the purposes of clarity, when this book uses the term *contacts,* it means people—your friends and colleagues. When it refers to *profiles,* it means the information you keep about friends and colleagues—phone numbers, email addresses, physical addresses, and so on.

Here's what Synergy imports during a sync (for more details, check out *http://tinyurl.com/ludxa3*):

- **Google.** Email messages, contacts (including Google Talk IM buddies), and calendar events, but not tasks.

- **Facebook.** Facebook contacts and events (However, this is a one-way affair: Contacts and events you add to Facebook show up in the Pre's Contacts and Calendar programs, but Synergy can't sync information you add to the Pre with Facebook because of restrictions imposed by the company).

- **Microsoft Exchange.** Email messages, contacts, calendar events, and tasks.

- **Email accounts.** Synergy syncs both POP and IMAP email accounts (for more on these types of account, see page 40), but not POP or IMAP contacts or calendars.

- **AOL IM (AIM).** Synergy adds AIM contacts to the Pre's contacts list, but it doesn't sync bi-directionally—any buddies you add to the Pre's Messenging program (see page 145) don't get synched back to AIM.

Note Microsoft Exchange is an email, calendar, and address book program issued to you by your employer. This type of account is typically harder to set up with the Pre than other types of accounts because you sometimes need your company's blessing to share the information with a handheld device and because there are arcane tech settings for servers and domains that you need to adjust. See page127 for details.

What Synergy Exports

Synergy doesn't export the information on your Pre across all your linked accounts when it performs a sync. If it did, you'd have information that you want to keep separate, like your friends' addresses in your Google account, propagated across all your linked accounts, such as your Microsoft Exchange work account.

Instead, when you send information from the Pre, whether that information is a new contact, a new email message, or a new calendar event, you select the account that you want the Pre to use for that outgoing information using a drop-down list, one that includes both your linked accounts as well as your Palm Profile account. If you don't select a specific account at all, the Pre uses your default account.

When you select a destination account in the Contacts and Calendar programs, the Pre adds that contact or calendar event to the named account. When you specify an account in the Email program, the Pre uses that account for your message's "From" address.

Your Default Account

Out of the box, your default account is the Palm Profile account. Any information you add to the Pre—when you add a new contact through the Pre's Contacts program, for example, or set up a calendar appointment in the All Calendars view—resides on the Pre only because your default account is the Palm Profile account; Synergy doesn't coordinate this information with any online account.

Once you add a linked account to your Pre in the Email, Calendar, or Contacts programs, that linked account becomes your default for new entries. But you can change the default account, and you can name a different default account each for the Contacts, Email, and Calendar programs. For example, if you use your Google calendar as your events bible, you probably want to make Google your default account for the Calendar program. That way, when you add an event in the Pre's All Calendars view, the Pre automatically adds that event to your Google calendar.

At the same time, you might make Microsoft Exchange the default account for the Pre's Contacts program. That way, when you add a new contact to the Pre without specifying a different account, Synergy exports it to your Microsoft Exchange account.

Note that when you use a default account that's different from Palm Profile, the information you add to the Pre gets saved to that default account only—the Pre doesn't back it up to your Palm Profile account (that account stores only the login information for your linked accounts, not the information in those accounts itself).

To change the default account within one of the Pre's applications, tap the application menu within the program, tap Preferences & Accounts, and, in the Contacts and Email programs, scroll to Default Account; in the Calendar application, scroll to Default Calendar. Tap the box for the current default account and then tap the name of the account you want to make the default from the drop-down list.

Set Up the Sync

The first step in syncing your Pre is importing information from your online accounts. When your Pre is new and you haven't added any email messages, contacts, calendar items, or tasks, the first time you sync, all the information flows one way: from your online accounts into the Pre. But over time, as you add contact info, calendar events, and to-do lists to your Pre, Synergy sync bi-directionally with your online accounts (either an account you specify or your default account).

To sync your phone and online accounts, your Pre needs to sign into your online services with your user name and password. You only have to provide sign-in information for each service once, and you can do so from any of the three Pre programs you sync—its Contacts, Calendar, and Email applications—which you'll learn more about later in the book. (Tasks get synced up, too, but you can't set up accounts in the Tasks application.)

> **Note** Though it depends on the number of contacts, calendar entries, to-do lists, and emails in your online accounts, your first sync will likely take longer than subsequent ones, because the first time out, Synergy needs to sync *all* your online information; later, it syncs only changes to that info.

Here's how to set up Synergy from the Contacts program:

❶ **Tap the Contacts icon in the Quick Launch panel.** If you've never synced an online account before, the Pre displays buttons for Google, Facebook, and Microsoft Exchange. Tap the account you want to sync (you have to sync them one at a time).

If you *have* synced a service before, the first step in syncing *another* service is a little different: Go into the Contacts application menu and tap Preference & Accounts→"Add an Account".

❷ **Tap Google, Facebook, or Microsoft Exchange.**

❸ **For Google and Facebook accounts, type in your user name and password.** You'll have to do the same for Exchange, too, but then you'll have to supply additional details, such as the *server* name (servers are big corporate computers that house information) for receiving email and the server's domain name, which is often the name of your company. You may have to check with one of your company's IT reps to get the information you need to sync your Exchange account.

④ **Tap Sign In.**

⑤ **The Pre accesses your account and automatically starts syncing your online info with all applicable Pre programs** (calendar events in the online account go to the Pre's Calendar program, profile information goes to Contacts on the Pre, and so on). As it syncs, the Pre displays a status message in the notification area that reads something like "Google: Syncing account."

⑥ **After the Pre finishes syncing, it displays a message like "Google sync complete!" along with the option to add another account or to tap Done.**

⑦ **Repeat this process for any other account (Google, Facebook, or Microsoft Exchange) you want to sync.**

Tip If you decide to permanently stop syncing your Pre with an online account such as Google, open Contacts, and then go to the application menu and tap Preferences & Account. Select the name of the account you want to remove (in this case, Google) by tapping it. A Change Login Settings screen comes up; on it, tap Remove Account.

Removing an account via the Contacts program only prevents your Pre from syncing your Contacts files—it continues to sync your email and calendar events with the same online service (in this example, Google). Deleting the account from Contacts only removes entries from your Pre—you're not deleting them from your Google account.

Work with Contact Information

Once you gather information on your friends and colleagues from multiple sources and the accounts are properly consolidated, you can view all of a given person's profile information—phone numbers, email addresses, IM contacts, physical addresses, and so on—in a single place without having to worry about overlap. The Pre won't list the same phone number twice, for example, even if it pulled that number from different sources. And if it finds, say, two different home phone numbers, it adds both to your contact's profile. Synergy automatically links the same people from different accounts so you won't have search multiple address books for, say, Jane Farrell's phone numbers and email addresses. In fact, the only way to tell where the information comes from—this piece from Facebook, that piece from Google—is when you edit profile information as explained below. And if Janie changes her number on Facebook, the Pre automatically applies the change to her profile page.

While you'll sync many kinds of information, contact info is the most complex, and because it involves so many small pieces, managing that information is more complex, too.

Tip When you first set up your Contacts (page 61), you get to choose a default account (Palm Profile, Google, Exchange) where all your new Contacts will end up. (If you don't choose an account, the Pre automatically picks your Palm Profile.) A brand-new contact added to the Pre gets synced *only* to this default account. To change the default account, open Contacts, go to the application menu and tap Preferences & Accounts→Default Account, and then tap the name of the account you want to make the default.

Link Contact Profiles

Synergy doesn't always sync perfectly. The Pre may not correctly link all the accounts for a single person. Syncing is an automated process: The Pre is supposed to recognize that your colleague Janie Farrell on Facebook is the same as the JJ Farrell in Google and Jane Farrell on Exchange. By comparing first and last names, mobile numbers, email accounts, and so on, the Pre gets it right most of the time, but mistakes are inevitable. And without your guidance, the Pre would have no way of knowing that it should combine the information for, say, Jane Farrell, if she uses her married name privately and her maiden name at work.

> **Tip** One of the entries you can add to a person's profile is a "Reminder" note. It might, for example, be an important question you want to ask this contact. When she calls you or sends you a message, or you call her, a notification appears at the bottom of the screen telling you that you created a reminder for her. Tap it to read the reminder.

To manually link address books, follow this example for Jane Farrell:

❶ Open Contacts and tap "Jane Farrell" (or however the name appears). Farrell's profile comes up with her name at the top.

❷ Tap Farrell's name. The Pre opens a mini-window that lists the sources of Farrell's contact info and offers you the option to link another profile to hers.

❸ Tap "Link more profiles."

❹ **The Pre switches to a screen that displays** *all* **your profiles.** Search for the profile you want to link to Farrell's and tap it. The Pre links that new profile and returns to Farrell's profile page, displaying the newly linked profile information under Farrell's name.

> **Note** When you link a profile, the Pre uses the name in the last linked profile as the name it displays in the Contacts list. So if you linked Jane Farrell's profile with one for Jane J. Farrell, Farrell's contact entry becomes Jane J. Farrell. You can change this by going into Farrell's profile page, tapping her name, selecting the Jane Farrell profile, and then selecting Set As Primary Profile.

You can easily tell if a contact has more than one profile linked to it: In the main Contacts list, a linked profile displays a stack of photos of the person (or a stack of silhouettes if you don't have a photo of that person). If you tap on that person's name to go to her profile page, the stack includes a circled number telling you how many profiles you linked to that person.

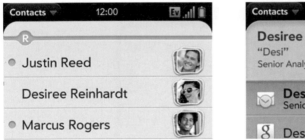 

Unlink a Profile

Unlinking a profile from one of your contacts is easy: Go to Contacts, tap the name of the person in question to bring up her profile page, and then tap her name at the top of the profile. The Pre displays a list of linked profiles. Tap the one you want to unlink, and then tap Unlink This Profile.

Add a Contact to the Pre

You meet people you want to add to your inner circle all the time. You can add them to your Pre's address book on-the-fly or, as explained on page 61, you can add them through the Phone program. In either case, Synergy adds their profiles to your default account on its next sync.

Here's how to add someone through the Contacts program:

❶ **Open Contacts.**

❷ **Tap the 👤⁺ icon.**

❸ **Type the person's name in the Name area.**

❹ **An icon for your default account appears beside the name.** If you want to add the contact to your default account, you can skip to the next step. To add the contact to a different linked account or to your Palm Profile account, tap the default-account icon and select the new account from the drop-down list.

> **Note** The only profile information from Facebook, Exchange, or Google that's backed up in your Palm Profile are the credentials for those accounts—namely, your Gmail user ID and password, and your Facebook user name. But you *can* use the Pre without syncing any of these services. If you do, then your contacts and calendar events are only backed up in your Palm Profile.

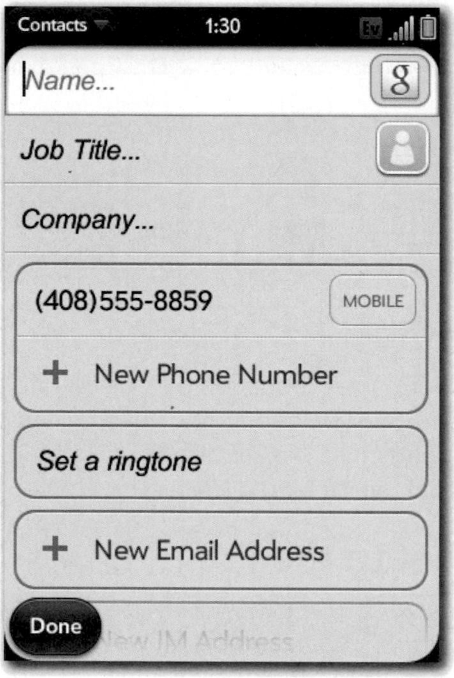

⑤ **Continue to enter as much or as little information about the person as you like.** You can enter multiple phone numbers, email addresses, ringtones, IM screen names, website addresses, reminders, notes, birthdays, spouse names, children's names, and nicknames. (You can add to or edit entries later, by tapping the Edit button at the bottom left-hand corner of a contact's profile page.)

⑥ **When everything looks good, tap Done.**

Sync manually

Once you enter a new contact, you can manually sync your Pre to bring it—and (in the case of your default account if it's not "Palm Profile") any corresponding online address book—up to date. You don't have to wait for the next scheduled automatic sync. That way, any contacts you add to the Pre show up in your default online account right away, and any contacts you add online (from any synced accounts) get imported into the Pre.

To manually sync accounts, open Contacts and then go to the application menu and tap Preferences & Accounts→Sync Now.

Remove a Profile or a Contact

Say you change careers, you break up with your honey, or you move halfway across the country so you don't need your gardener anymore. To clean up your address book, you can remove contacts two ways:

- **To delete a contact with no links or to delete a contact** *and* **all of its links,** go to the person's profile, open the application menu, and then tap Delete Contact→Delete All Profiles.

- **To delete just one profile in a linked contact,** tap the contact name to open a list of that person's profiles. Then tap the entry you want to deep-six and tap Delete This Profile.

> **Note** If you delete someone's profile on your Pre and it's associated with an online account, Synergy also removes the profile from the online account. But you can't remove Facebook contacts from the Pre without removing the Facebook account from your phone altogether. The only way to remove a single Facebook contact from the Pre is to remove that contact from Facebook itself. The Pre will reflect the change the next time Synergy syncs accounts. Same goes for IM contacts. You can view your IM buddies on the Pre, but you can't add or remove them from buddy lists. You can only do that from a desktop computer, though changes made there will show up on the Pre after a sync.

Customize Contact Display Order

The Pre automatically displays your contacts by last name, but you can have it sort your contacts by first name (Mary) and then last name (Smith), or by company name. If you choose the latter, the Pre sorts by company name in ascending order (A to Z, so Alpha Co. will appear before Zeta, Inc.). And within each company, the Pre can sort your contacts by first name then last name, or by last name then first name.

To sort your contacts, go to the Contacts application menu and tap Preferences & Accounts→List Order.

Add a Contact to the Launcher

If you get in touch with certain people all the time, you may want to add them to the Launcher so their profiles are always just a tap away. To do that, open the Contacts program, tap the person's name to bring up his screen, and then open the application menu and tap "Add to Launcher."

You can give the person a label, like "Concierge" or "Messenger Service," on the next screen. If the person's profile includes a picture (see page 214), it becomes the Launcher icon. Otherwise you see a silhouette for that person.

You remove a contact from the Launcher by tapping "Remove from Launcher" in the application menu. Alternatively, hold the orange key and tap the contact, and then tap Delete.

Merge Calendars

Just as Synergy consolidates profiles from different online address books into a single profile on the Pre, it also syncs calendars from different sources with your Pre calendar. If you have a calendar on Google, in Facebook, or in Microsoft Exchange ActiveSync, your Pre assembles all your events in one place and color-codes them to show which calendar they came from. Alternatively, you can view each imported calendar separately.

To see an individual calendar, tap the oval in the upper-right corner of the calendar display. The word "ALL" should be in that oval to indicate that you're looking at a consolidated view of your calendars. From the list that appears, tap the name of the calendar you want to look at on its own (Google, Facebook, Exchange, or Palm Profile).

If you add an event to your consolidated calendar, the Pre adds that event to your synced default calendar, too (except for Facebook).

You'll learn how to schedule events, set alarms, and more in Chapter 5.

> **Tip** The Facebook calendar sync, as with Facebook contacts, is a one-way affair: Events you add to Facebook's calendar online show up in the Calendar app on the Pre, but adding calendar events to the Pre won't add them to the online Facebook calendar.

Combine Email Accounts

Synergy syncs email messages, too. You can see all your messages in one universal inbox, or view the accounts separately. When you compose a new message, the Pre lists all the email addresses you have on file for that recipient so you can choose just where you want your note sent. It also lets you choose which of your own email addresses you want to send the email *from*. A complete discussion of email starts on page 125.

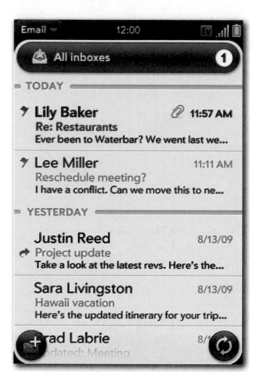

Sync with a Desktop PC

Synergy's always-connected status means the info on your Pre is always up to date with your online accounts. But what about information you don't store online, like names, addresses, and phone numbers on your desktop or laptop PC? You might want a way to sync your Pre with data sequestered on your hard drive.

Fortunately, you've got a couple of ways to do that. One lets you sync regularly, just as you do with Synergy, and the other lets you update your Pre manually. Both of them involve a little extra work, however.

Sync Automatically

If you use contact programs like Outlook on a Windows machine or iCal on a Mac and you'd like to go right on using them with your Pre, the good news is that you can. The bad news is that you may have to spend some money on third-party software to keep the relationship going.

The methods listed below let you sync contacts, calendar events, and tasks on your Windows or Mac PC with your Pre. The first two options work on the same principle: They send information from your computer to Google, and Synergy takes over from there, syncing your Google account with your Pre. The last option uses a wireless network connection, like a home or office network.

- **If you have a Windows XP or Vista PC,** try Google Sync, which syncs your Outlook calendar with your Google Calendar. It's a free option worth checking out at *google.com/sync*.

- CompanionLink Software sells a $30 application that syncs Microsoft Outlook contacts, calendar events, tasks, and notes with your Google account. A separate $30 program syncs Palm Desktop contacts, calendar events, tasks, and memos with your Google account. (Palm Desktop is the organizer software that Palm supplies with its Treo smartphones and PDAs—personal digital assistants.) Head to *www.companionlink.com/products/companionlinkforgoogle.html* for details.

- **If you have a Mac,** Google offers a Google Sync application that keeps iCal in sync with Google Calendar and the Mac Address Book. And Palm recommends Sync'Em to keep the Mac Address Book in sync with Gmail contacts; check it out at *Syncem.com*.

- You can also **sync Windows PCs over a wireless network.** Download PocketMirror for Outlook (*www.chapura.com/pre*; you can download a trial version in the App Catalog). It syncs contacts and calendar events between Outlook and the Pre. It works with Outlook by itself or with Outlook and the Microsoft Exchange servers in your office.

Sync Manually

You may want to get information from your PC or Mac once and be done with it. To do that, you need Palm's Data Transfer Assistant. Download it for free from *http://tinyurl.com/n8zxud*. Palm offers versions for both Windows PCs and Macs, and both versions use the Pre's USB cable to connect your smartphone and computer.

> **Note** On a Windows Vista or XP machine, the Data Transfer Assistant works with Outlook 2003 or Outlook 2007. On a Mac (OS X 10.5 or later), it works to transfer contacts from Address Book or calendar entries from iCal.

You can transfer information to Google, Microsoft Exchange, or to your Palm Profile. Once you decide, Data Transfer Assistant does all the heavy lifting in the background. The transfer can take up to 10 minutes, and you won't receive any status reports—you'll only see a message when the transfer is complete. The program works application-by-application, starting with Contacts, then Calendars, and finishing up (on a Windows PC) with Tasks and Memos.

Remember, this is a one-time, one-way, transfer tool for people making the transition to Palm's new Internet-based webOS software. If you want to continue syncing with a PC or Mac, try one of the third-party approaches listed above. Otherwise, your syncing days with the Palm Desktop or Outlook applications will be history.

> **Tip** While you *can* use the Data Transfer Assistant (DTA) more than once to transfer contacts, calendar events, and tasks to your phone, you probably don't want to. Here's why: DTA isn't synching software, it's simply a batch-transfer program. Each time you use DTA, it transfers all your contacts, calendars, and tasks, both new ones and those you transferred previously. Therefore, you'll end up with duplicate entries, and these duplicates may show up in the relevant applications on your phone. For example, in John Smith's profile, you might see the same work phone number listed twice.

Chapter

4

The Pre as Phone

Whatever else the Pre may be—and it's many things, as you'll see in the following chapters—at its core, it's a phone. And because it's a smartphone, the Pre is loaded with features that standard cellphones lack, such as the ability to call phone numbers embedded in a web page, or to find contacts and phone numbers with just a few keystrokes.

In this chapter, you'll learn to use your Pre to make and receive calls, add contacts via the Phone program, set up and use voicemail, assign ringtones, and more.

Make a Phone Call

The Pre gives you a whopping *six* ways to make a phone call, using everything from a traditional dial pad to embedded phone numbers.

Dialing

You can dial a number using the Pre's physical keyboard, which slides out from under the phone, or with the Pre's onscreen "virtual" dial pad, called the dial pad, which responds to your touch.

From the keyboard

If you prefer tactile feedback when you dial a number, your only option is the Pre's physical keyboard. It integrates a standard set of keys into its traditional QWERTY layout, with the numbers 0 through 9 piggybacking on letter keys and highlighted in orange.

Dialing from the keyboard offers one big advantage over the Pre's on-screen dial pad: You don't have to open the Pre's phone program before you start dialing. The Pre is a *smart*phone, after all, and when you start dialing from the keyboard in Card view or from the Launcher, the Pre knows you're entering a phone number. It pops up a window displaying the number as you type, and when you're done, you just tap the number to dial.

Note As the phone calls one of your contacts, it displays a picture of the person you're calling, providing his or her mug is in that person's profile (see page 214).

Once you dial a number, the Pre checks it against your Contacts list. If it finds a match, it displays a link to that person's profile. You can tap the link to go to the profile, to get an alternate phone number, for example.

Use the Dial Pad

You can enter a phone number using the Pre's onscreen dial pad, too. First, open the Phone application by tapping the Quick Launch panel's phone icon.

The dial pad uses a standard dialing configuration and has three buttons underneath.

> **Tip** The Pre's onscreen keys are large enough so you can dial with one hand. Just grip the Pre in your palm, and let your thumb do the number-tapping.

The largest of the three (running the width of the dial pad) has a phone icon; tap it to connect your calls.

The smaller button on the left, which looks like a pair of upside-down eyeglasses, takes you to voicemail, which you'll learn about later in this chapter (on page 88).

The button on the right opens your call history, a list of all the calls you made or received. (You'll learn how to make calls from the Call History screen in a moment.) From the Call History screen, tap the dial pad button to return to the dial pad. (It's in the same place the Call History button was.)

To make a call, enter the phone number using the dial pad (as soon as you start entering a number, the voicemail and Call History buttons disappear). With every key strike, the Pre emits a beep and displays the corresponding number in the window above the dial pad. If you make a mistake, tap the onscreen backspace key to remove the last digit. To delete the *entire* number, hold down the onscreen backspace key.

> **Tip** You can copy and paste (see page 45) numbers from other applications, like Memo and Contacts, into the dial pad.

When you finish entering the number, tap the phone icon to place your call.

> **Tip** If you get a busy signal and want to try calling again, open the Phone application and tap the phone icon ☏. When you do, the number or name of the person you last dialed appears above the dial pad. Simply tap the same phone icon again to call the number. This redial shortcut is handy when you're trying to get through to a talk show's call-in line or to vote for your favorite singer on *American Idol*.

Automated Dialing

Of course, typing even 10 digits seems so 20th-century. Your Pre can automate dialing in a number of ways. As you'll learn in the next few pages, you can call from your Call History or Contacts list, use a speed-dial number, or tap a number in a web page.

> **Note** Thanks to its proximity sensor (see page 21), you won't inadvertently tap any buttons on the Pre's screen when you hold the phone to your ear. The screen temporarily shuts down and automatically wakes up when you put the phone down.

By Call History

As you learned above, the Call History screen lists all the calls you've made, fielded, or missed. To see this list, go to the Quick Launch panel and tap the phone icon, and then tap the Call History button.

You can tell what kind of call each item in the list is by the color and direction of the arrow beside each phone number. Calls that you made have a green arrow that points right, calls you received have a blue arrow that points left, and calls you missed have a broken red arrow.

Tip To see just your missed calls so you can prioritize callbacks, tap Missed Calls at the top of the Call History list.

You'll probably see different kinds of entries, too: some that are just phone numbers, others that are names instead of numbers, others that say "Blocked number," and still others that are names accompanied by photographs. The kind of entry you see depends on what's in your Contacts list, because your Pre checks phone numbers against that list. So if a call comes in from some-one in your Contacts list, the Pre displays the name of the person and a pho-tograph of her—if you've added one to her profile, that is—instead of her phone number.

To call any of the numbers in this list, simply tap the number or name.

Dial by Contact

The last chapter taught you how to import and create profiles in your Contacts list. You can call anyone on that list by pulling up their profile page and tapping one of their phone numbers (mobile, work, home, and so on). You can get to a person's contact screen three ways:

- **Universal search.** In Card view or the Launcher, start typing the first or last name of the person you want to call. You can also type the initials of the person you want to call or a nickname (like "Dad") that you've added to the person's profile. Matching names pop up as you type, and you can select a name any time (the name you want often appears before you finish typing) by tapping it. Once you do, that person's contact info comes up, listing all his phone numbers. Tap the one you want to call.

- **From within the Phone application.** You can call up the Contacts screen by tapping the ▣ icon in the upper-right corner of the screen, just above the dial pad. This isn't your full master Contacts list; only contacts with phone numbers turn up here. You can flick or scroll through the list, but that's not a very quick way to find a number. It's faster to use the Pre's handy search box at the top of the list—start typing in a first or last name, and the list displays only items that match what you enter.

- **Open the Contacts application.** As always, you can open Contacts from the Quick Launch panel to see all your contacts. You won't see a search box when the program opens, but if you start pressing letters on the keyboard, one appears onscreen. Start typing in the name of the person you want to find.

Add contacts via the Phone program

You can add people to your Contacts list from the phone program in several ways.

To create a contact based on a call you made or received, go to the Call History screen (see page 77). If the Pre hasn't matched a number with your Contacts list, it displays the number with a silhouette and a + sign beside it. That's your invitation to add that person to your Contacts list; page 63 has the details about how to do that.

You can create a contact as you're making a call, too. Do one of the following:

- **After you type a number into the dial pad,** tap the "Add to Contacts" button at the bottom of the screen. (This button replaces the usual buttons—shown on page 76—the moment you tap a number.) The Pre takes you to a screen with three options:

  — If the contact is new, tap Save As New and enter the name, title, company, email address, and other profile info on the screen that appears. The phone number you typed in to make the call is already filled in. You can add other phone numbers to the profile as well.

  — If want to add the number to one of your existing contacts, tap "Add to Existing", and then tap the person's name when the Contacts list pops up.

  — Tap Dismiss if you change your mind.

- **While you're on a call to a new number,** the silhouette of a person with a + sign appears beside the number. Tap it and follow the process listed above to save a new contact, add to an existing one, or cancel.

Use Speed Dial

Save yourself some time and effort by assigning speed-dial keys to people you talk to frequently. That way, you only have to enter a few keystrokes to call them—the Pre automatically opens the Phone program and dials the number.

> **Note** You can't use the 1 key to speed-dial anyone. The Pre reserves this key for speed-dialing your voicemail account.

You can assign speed-dial keys to a maximum of 26 people. Here's how:

❶ **Open Contacts (in the Quick Launch panel, tap the Contacts icon).**

❷ **Use universal search (see page 46) to find the person's name, or scroll to his name and open his profile.**

❸ **Open the application menu in the upper-left corner of the screen.**

> **Note** Remember, to open the application menu in any program, tap the program's name on the left side of the status bar.

❹ **Tap Set Speed Dial.** A profile screen showing the contact's phone numbers pops up. Tap the phone number you want to assign to the speed-dial key.

❺ **Assign an available speed-dial key from the list that appears.** You may have to scroll through the list to find the key you want.

Reassign a speed-dial key

You can only have 26 speed-dial numbers, one for each letter of the alphabet. If you run out, congratulations on having so many friends! You can always reassign a key if you start calling someone else more than the person that key is dedicated to now. Simply repeat the steps above for your new contact. Once you type in the already-reserved speed-dial key, the Pre double-checks that you want to make the switch.

Don't feel obligated to keep a person on speed dial if you don't call him very often. In Contacts, pull up the profile for the person who's about to lose his speed-dialing status, open the application menu, and tap Set Speed Dial. Then tap the onscreen listing that appears with the phone number that has a speed-dial key (you don't tap the actual key on the keyboard). Tap the Remove Speed Dial button that appears above a list of all the letters already assigned to people and available as speed-dial keys.

Call a speed-dial number

To call someone with a speed-dial number, go to Card view, the Launcher, or the Phone program, and then press and hold the speed-dial key you assigned to that person. An instant later, the Pre dials the number. Easy, huh?

> **Tip** If you tap but don't *hold* a speed-dial key, you still have the option of speed-dialing the person. That's because once you tap a key, the Pre goes into universal search mode. So if you tap, say, the G key, the Pre displays a list that includes the person you assigned that speed-dial key to, along with things like Google Maps.

Dial from a Web Page or Email Message

Your Pre's designed to dial phone numbers that appear in web pages, text messages, and email messages. If the number is underlined on the Pre's screen, the phone recognizes it. Tap it and the Pre opens the Phone program and enters the number; tap the phone icon to make the call.

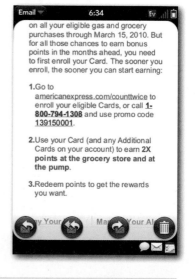

9-1-1 Calls

If your Pre is locked (see page 7) and you've set it up so you have to enter a four-digit PIN or more secure password to unlock it (page 244 tells you how to do that), but you're in trouble and need to dial 9-1-1, you don't have to go through the rigmarole of entering the security code to start dialing. You can quickly place that emergency call: Just press the power button to wake up the phone, and either slide the keyboard out, or drag the padlock up to unlock the screen (you don't need to enter your PIN or password). The Pre displays a button labelled "Emergency Call." Tap it and the Pre opens the dial pad with 9-1-1 already entered. Tap the phone icon ✆ to make the call.

Intra-Office Dialing

If you call coworkers from your office phone by dialing a four-digit extension, you can enjoy the same privilege with your Pre. You just need to set up your Pre so that, when you enter a four-digit number and press the Call button, it adds the area code and the *exchange* (the first three numbers of a phone number) before it dials that four-digit extension, saving you a lot of typing.

For example, if the phone number for Joe in Accounting is 1-212-555-1234, you can tell the Pre that when you enter *1234* (his extension) and then tap the phone icon ✆ , you want it to add the first six digits of the number (212555). From that point on, when you enter *1234* and tap the ✆ icon, the Pre dials 1-212-555-1234 (it adds the first 1 automatically). Here's how:

❶ **Open the Phone program by tapping the phone icon in the Quick Launch panel.**

❷ **Open the program's application menu by tapping the upper-left corner of the screen, and then tap Preferences.** The phone dialer screen moves aside, and the Phone Preferences card slides up to replace it.

❸ **In the Dialing Shortcuts box, tap "Add new number".** The Dialing Shortcuts screen pops up.

❹ **Tap the When I Dial box, and tell the Pre how many digits you'll enter when you want it to automatically dial a full number.** In the example above, you'd enter *4* here because you want the Pre to dial Joe's full number when you type in his four-digit extension (1234). You can trigger a dialing shortcut with a minimum of four digits and a maximum of seven.

Dialing Shortcuts

WHEN I DIAL

4 digits

USE THIS DIALING PREFIX

Enter number

These shortcuts are digits added to the
beginning of the number you are
attempting to call
Example: (510) 123-XXXX

Done

⑤ **In the Use This Dialing Prefix box, enter the digits that you want the Pre to dial when you enter a shortcut number.** For Joe's number, you want your phone to dial his area code and exchange before it dials his extension, so you enter *212555* (you don't need to enter the 1 because the Pre adds that to the beginning of the number automatically). If you chose a different number in the When I Dial box in step 4, you'll need to enter fewer numbers here.

⑥ **Tap Done.** From now on you'll save your fingers some work.

Overseas Calling

In the U.S., your Pre works on a speedy *CDMA* (Code Division Multiple Access) cellular network run by Sprint. Sprint has made *roaming* arrangements with overseas phone companies, so you can call friends in Paris or wherever, and you can call home to the U.S. while you travel abroad. (See page 101 for more about roaming.) You'll pay handsomely for the privilege, of course.

Voice calls from Brazil to the U.S., for example, cost $1.99 per minute, while voice calls from China to the States are $2.99 per minute. And you can pay as much as *$4.99* per minute to call the States from Vietnam. Taxes and surcharges may be tacked on by the host country, too. See *http://tinyurl.com/mslp89* for details on traveling internationally.

You'll pay through the nose to make the odd call from the U.S. *to* these or other countries on the Pre as well, though rates aren't quite as onerous. Calls to Brazil are $1.49 to $1.71 per minute (depending on whether you're calling a landline or mobile phone). Calls to China and Vietnam are $1.49 to $1.52 per minute. If you regularly call overseas, consider Sprint's $4-per-month International Long Distance Plan, which lowers the per-country rates considerably. Sprint also has a plan catering to folks who frequently call Mexico. For details on all the international rate plans from the U.S, go to *http://tinyurl.com/lzwx73*.

Of course, in many overseas areas, you'll still be able to exploit WiFi for a data connection, though data rates can also be oppressive. (Check the websites mentioned above for details.) And as of this writing, you *can't* exploit an internet connection to make cheap calls back to the U.S. using VOIP (Voice over Internet Protocol) technology.

If you call overseas from the U.S., type the + sign at the beginning of the number, and the Pre automatically adds the 011 prefix. Then add the country code (found on the Sprint sites or Google), city or area code, and finally the local number. (If you're making a call from somewhere else in the world where the dialing prefix differs, you need to type in the *whole* number, since the 011 prefix won't apply.)

Incoming Calls

With a Pre, you rarely have to answer a call without knowing who's on the other end. If a custom ringtone (see below) doesn't reveal who the caller is, a picture on the screen just might. Knowing who the caller is, you can decide whether to answer a call or let it go to voicemail.

Answer a Call

When someone calls you, all the info the Pre knows about that person (her name, number, a photo, and so on) shows up on the Pre's screen. If you want to talk to the person, you can field a call three ways:

- **If the screen is dark,** you have two options: Drag up the green phone icon that appears on the bottom of the screen (similar to the way you unlock the phone), or slide open the keyboard. Either way, to confirm that you've just answered the call, the Pre displays the call screen shown on page 90.

- **If you're working on the phone,** a green Answer icon and a red Ignore icon pop up along with the caller's name and number (if known), along with her picture (if you have one on the Pre). This info takes over the bottom half of the screen; the upper half is reserved for whichever application you were using before the call came in. If the name, number, and caller ID info aren't known, the same icons appear with the words "Unknown Caller" or "Blocked Number". This type of notification grabs a far narrower slice of the bottom of the screen. Either way, tap the green icon to answer the call; when you're done, press the red button to hang up.

- **If you have the Pre's earbuds on** (see page 3), press the Answer/End Call button on the headset cord to take the call. The Pre pauses whatever you're listening to or watching when you make or receive a call, and picks up the beat where you left off when you hang up. (You use this same button for call waiting—see page 91). If you use third-party headphones, you have to answer the call by tapping the phone icon.

  When you answer with a wired headset, a headphone icon appears in the bottom-left corner of the call screen. Tap that icon to switch to the speaker-phone (see page 91) or to a TTY machine (see page 105).

Ignore a Call

If a call comes in that you don't want to take, you can send it to voicemail in several ways:

- **Let it ring.** After about 30 seconds, the call goes to voicemail. This strat-egy's only downside is that you have to put up with the ringer for half a minute, which can seem like hours if you're trying to concentrate on something else.

- **Press the center button.** The phone goes silent on your end, but your caller continues to hear the phone ring until the call goes to voicemail a half-minute later.

In both the above cases, the Pre displays a Missed Call notifica-tion with the caller's name, phone number, and picture (if available). You can tap the large green "Call back" button to do just that, or the gray-and-black Dismiss button to get rid of the notification. (If the Pre doesn't recognize the caller, you only see the Dismiss button.) If you don't do anything, these notifications eventually turn into small icons on the right side of the notifications area. Tap an icon to summon details of the call.

If you tap the notifications area above the "Call back" or Dismiss buttons, the Pre displays the caller's contact info so you can choose how to respond (by email, text, or by calling a specific number).

• **Press the red hang-up button, or press the power button twice.** This time the call goes to voicemail and you'll get an Ignored Call notification that disappears after a few seconds.

Go to Voicemail

When someone leaves you a message, the Pre displays a voicemail icon in the notifications area. The icon includes a blue circle with a number in it, which tells you how many messages await your attention.

To listen to your messages, tap the voicemail icon below the dial pad, or press the 1 key on the Pre's keyboard.

Set up voicemail

The first time you access voicemail, a friendly automated voice guides you through the setup process. You need to:

- Choose an easy-to-remember but hard-to-guess four- to seven-digit passcode.

- Record your first and last name.

- Record a greeting.

- Decide whether you want to enter a passcode each time you call voicemail from your Pre or to bypass this security feature and go directly to your messages. Either way, you have to enter your passcode when you check voicemail from another phone.

Listen to voicemail

The Pre's voicemail system works like most others—voice prompts guide you through your messages one by one.

> **Note** If the Pre is lacking anywhere compared with the iPhone, it's in voicemail. The iPhone has a clever feature called Visual Voicemail that displays the names and numbers of the people who've left you messages, so you can review the list *without* calling in to voicemail to listen to your messages. And you can select any message you want to listen to, rather than having to review them in chronological order. You can't do either of those things on the Pre.

To listen to a message, tap 1. You can repeat the message (tap 1-1), save it (tap 9), or delete it (tap 7). When you call into voicemail, you have other options, too: You can change your greeting by tapping 3, or tap 4 to go into a "personal options" menu to do things like rerecord your name or change your voicemail password.

> **Tip** Sometimes the Pre can be a little slow about resetting your voicemail count to zero after you listen to and erase all your messages. If this happens, go to the Phone program's application menu and tap Preferences →Voicemail Count Reset to wipe the slate clean.

Phone Features

Once you connect to a call, the Pre's screen changes to include additional on-call options.

The first three are pretty self-explanatory:

- **Audio.** Free up your hands or let another person in on the conversation with the Pre's built-in speakerphone. Tap the onscreen Audio button to turn the feature on or off.

> **Tip** If a caller on speakerphone tells you he hears an echo, turn the phone face-down (with the screen facing the table). The Pre's speaker is on the backside of the device, so this should fix the problem.

- **Mute.** Tapping Mute turns the Pre's microphone off so a caller can't hear your end of the conversation. Tap Mute again to turn the mic back on.

- **Key pad.** You'll encounter more menus to navigate automated directories than you ever will walking through the restaurant section of a mall. To wend your way through, you need to press a variety of touch tones. That's where the Pre's Key Pad button comes in. Even if you dialed out using the dial pad, it disappears once the call goes through. To bring it back, tap the Key Pad button (even though Palm calls the onscreen dialer a "dial pad" everywhere else, it calls it a "key pad" here).

Manage More Than One Call at a Time

There's a fourth icon that appears onscreen when you're on a call: the Add Call icon ✆. It's a little more complex than the other three, because it opens the door to several types of calls.

Here are your options:

- **Take a second call.** If another call comes in while you're on the phone, the Pre sounds a call-waiting beep. To take the new call and put the original caller on hold, tap the green phone icon. Or you can tap the red button ✆ to send the call to voicemail; or simply ignore the beeps, and the call goes to voicemail in 30 seconds.

  If you decide to take the second call, you can switch between the two. When you tap the green phone icon to answer the second call, the Pre splits the main screen vertically and displays the first caller's name and number on top, and the second caller's name and number on the bottom. You can tell which person you're talking to because you'll see a clock timing the call next to the active line's number, and the words "On hold" next to the other person's number.

  To switch between them, tap the double arrows that appear on the screen between the two calls, or tap the words "On hold". Either way, the person you were just talking to gets put on hold, and the other caller now has your undivided attention.

- **Make a conference call.** Suppose you take a call from your boss, and now you need to coordinate plans with a colleague. Maybe you want to talk to them individually, or make this into a conference call. While still talking to your boss, tap the Add Call button. The familiar dial pad appears, and you can keep on chatting by speakerphone. Dial the second number and then tap 📞. When that caller picks up, the Pre places your boss on hold. Now you have two options: You can either tap End All Calls to hang up on both people, or make this into a conference call so everyone can chat. To merge the calls, tap the upward-pointing Conference button. The words "Conference Call" appears onscreen.

When everyone has gotten a word in edgewise, you can end the call by tapping the red End button. Or, if one of the callers hangs up, you're back to chatting with the other person.

Multitask During a Call

Your Pre is a mean multitasking machine, but—at least while you're on the phone—it has its limits. That's because Sprint's networks don't permit what's called "simultaneous voice and data," which means you can't carry on a conversation *and* send email messages, surf the Web, or send photos at the same time.

Sprint's network handles your voice, but your "data" (the email messages, web page requests, photos, and so on) needs its own line of communication. And there's only one place your Pre can get that second line: in a WiFi hotspot (see page 155). Find one of those and you can chat and check your email, browse the Web, and share vacation photos (see page 217) all at once.

> **Tip** The only time you have to be in a WiFi hotspot to send and receive data is when you're on the phone. If you're not using the phone, the Pre can use the voice line for data.

There's one exception to the multitasking limit: text messages (page 146). Since text messages use the voice network, you can send and receive texts while you talk, without the need for a WiFi connection.

Send a Message to the Person You're Talking To

Sometimes when you're on a call, you want to share a document like a Word file or a photo. Rather than wait until you hang up, you can tap the center button to enter Card view (page 36), open Contacts from the Quick Launch panel, and then tap the name of the person you're talking to. This opens his profile, where you can tap the appropriate contact option to send him a text message or email.

Ringtones

The Pre comes with 10 ringtones, including an old telephone ring, a rain dance, and a dulcimer. You can choose one of these as your standard ring, create your own custom ringtones, or assign specific rings to people.

Assign a Ringtone to All Calls

Here's how to pick which sound you want the Pre to use as the standard ring:

 Open the Launcher and tap Sounds & Ringtones. The icon looks like a loudspeaker.

❷ **Tap the name of the ringtone that's listed under Ringer Switch On.** (If this is your first visit to Sounds & Ringtones, the "Pre" ringtone is listed—it sounds like wind chimes.) When you tap it, you're taken to a screen that lists all the ringtones on your Pre, with a checkmark next to the selected tone.

❸ **To listen to a ringtone, tap the play button to the right of its name.** You can stop the preview by tapping the stop button that replaces the play button.

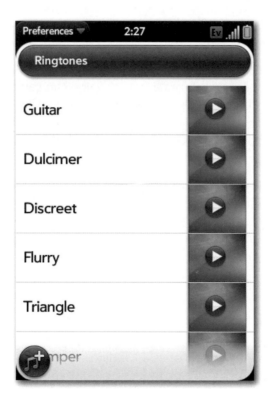

❹ **Once you find a ringtone you like, tap its name to select it.** The Pre brings you back to the main Sounds & Ringtones screen, which now lists the ringtone you picked.

❺ **To control how loud the ring is, drag the Ringtone Volume slider in the middle of the Sounds & Ringtones screen (dragging right makes it louder, left quieter).** The Pre plays your ringtone as you drag, so you can find just the right volume.

Select a Ringtone from Your Music Collection

Ten ringtones isn't a whole lot to choose from. Happily, Palm lets you use any of the audio (music) files on your Pre as a ringtone.

To do so, follow steps 1 and 2 above. On the Ringtones screen, tap the "Add a Ringtone" icon in the bottom-left corner of the screen (it looks like two musical notes with a + sign next to them). The Pre lists all your audio files.

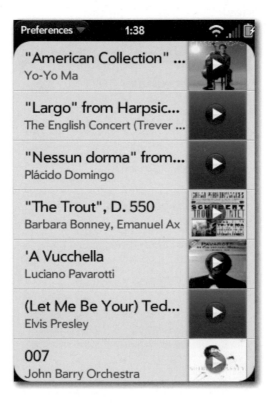

Scroll up or down the list until you find one you like, tap the play button to preview it, and then tap the song's name to make it your ringtone.

Tip You can copy ringtones from your desktop PC to your Pre via the USB connector (see page 9). Imported ringtones get stored with all your other ringtones and don't appear in the music library (see page 192).

Assign Ringtones to Contacts

Some songs make great ringtones for friends and family (*He Ain't Heavy He's My Brother* and *Mamma Mia* spring to mind). To assign a ringtone to one of your contacts, follow these steps:

❶ **Open Contacts and scroll down to the person you're assigning the ringtone to.**

❷ **Tap Edit in the bottom-left corner of the screen.**

❸ **Tap "Set a ringtone", and the Pre takes you to the now-familiar list of all your ringtones.**

❹ **Tap the ringtone you want and then tap Done.**

If you change your mind and want to unassign or reassign a ringtone, just follow steps 1 and 2 again, and then tap the box showing the ringtone you assigned. Then either tap Change Ringtone and pick a new tone from the ringtone list, or tap Delete Ringtone to unassign it from that person. Finally, tap Done. If you delete a custom ringtone from a contact, the Pre uses your standard ringtone for him or her.

Silence Your Phone

When you're in a movie theater or meeting, you don't want your phone to make a sound. To shut off the ringer, slide the ringer switch (on top of the phone) to the right until you can see red underneath the switch. Now if someone calls you, the Pre won't make a ringing sound.

Depending on how you've got things set up in Sounds & Ringtones, the phone may still vibrate, even when the ringer is off. If you want the phone to vibrate when the ringer is off and a call comes in, open the Launcher and go to Sounds & Ringtones. Then drag the Vibrate switch to the On position. Keep in mind that people may hear (and get annoyed by) the buzzing sound the phone makes when it vibrates.

Hands-Free Calling

"Bluetooth" may sound like a tragic dental condition, but it's actually a cool technology that lets you receive phone calls on a wireless headset, so you can do things like keep your hands on the wheel while driving. (As of this writing, the Pre doesn't have voice dialing, so you can't *place* a call using a Bluetooth headset.)

Bluetooth devices communicate with the Pre from as far as 30 feet away, though it's hard to imagine many circumstances where your Pre would be that far away. If you're walking along with a Bluetooth headset clipped to your ear, the Pre is likely in your pocket or handbag. In the car, you might put it in the glove compartment or on the seat next to you.

Tip You can listen to music on your Pre with a wireless *stereo* Bluetooth headset, but not with a mono model.

You see Bluetooth in action all the time, most notably when you spot someone in a car or walking down the street who seems to be talking to himself until you spy a little earpiece on his ear. To become one of those people, you need to set up your Pre to work with a Bluetooth headset, earpiece, or car kit that you buy separately. This section explains how to configure one.

Note If you're strapped for cash and don't want to shell out for a Bluetooth headset, you can at least *receive* calls using the corded earbuds that come with the Pre. Just press the button on the cord when a call comes in, and you can chat hands-free. (Unfortunately, you can't *place* calls using the earbuds.)

Add a Bluetooth Device

Before you can use a Bluetooth headset, you need to "pair" it with your Pre, that is, establish an exclusive relationship between the two. Otherwise, anyone wandering around with a Bluetooth device could answer your phone, eavesdrop on your calls, or call Bora Bora on your dime.

Note The Pre is compatible with lots of different Bluetooth headsets and car kits. Check out *http://tinyurl.com/kqjyql* for a list.

The exact pairing process depends on what kind of Bluetooth device you get, but here's a general overview:

❶ **Turn on your Bluetooth earpiece by following the manufacturer's instructions.** Once it's on, the earpiece starts emitting a silent signal that your Pre can detect.

❷ **On the Pre, tap the upper-right corner of the screen to summon the connection menu.**

❸ **In the menu, tap Bluetooth→"Turn on Bluetooth".** The tiny Bluetooth indicator ✳ appears.

❹ **Tap the upper-right corner of the screen to bring up the connection menu again.**

⑤ **In the menu, tap Bluetooth Preferences→"Add device".** This tells your Pre to "listen" for Bluetooth signals like the one coming from the earpiece.

The Pre displays a list of Bluetooth devices it finds; tap on the one you want to pair with your Pre. When you do that, the Pre displays a spinning circle as it goes about its mating dance, and the Bluetooth earpiece may respond, perhaps by blinking or lighting up.

⑥ **After your Pre and the earpiece get to know each other, the Pre may prompt you to enter a passcode.** If not, the devices are already paired, so you can skip to the next step.

Some Bluetooth devices come with preset passcodes that you need to enter to pair the device. Others let you make up your own passcode. Check the instructions that came with your device to see what it requires. If you need to enter a pre-set passcode, read the instructions to find out where to find the passcode and how to enter it.

⑦ **You'll know the devices are paired when you see a little phone icon next to the earpiece's name on the Pre.** You can now answer calls with your earpiece—check the manufacturer's instructions to learn how.

End Your Bluetooth Relationship

All good things come to an end, and at some point you may decide to ditch your Bluetooth earpiece or car kit for a new model. You have two ways to make your Pre bid farewell to a Bluetooth device.

First, go to a list of your Bluetooth devices. Tap the Bluetooth icon in the Launcher, and then tap the switch so that Bluetooth is on. You can also tap the connection menu in the upper-right corner of the Pre's screen, tap Bluetooth→Bluetooth Preferences, and then tap the switch so that Bluetooth is on. The Pre displays a list of all the Bluetooth devices your Pre knows about. From there you can:

- **Delete a device.** To *permanently* "unpair" a Bluetooth device (so your Pre no longer recognizes it), find the one you want to remove and drag it off the screen to the right. When the Pre asks for confirmation, tap Delete to make the divorce final, or Cancel if you change your mind.

Tip This kind of divorce isn't necessarily forever. If you have second thoughts, you can always rekindle the relationship, and pair up the devices again by following the instructions on page 98.

- **Disconnect from a Bluetooth device.** Though you can have more than one Bluetooth device paired with your Pre, you can only use one such device at a time, which is where this option comes in handy: It's more like a temporary separation than a divorce. From the list of Bluetooth devices, tap the currently connected device to disconnect it so you can pair another Bluetooth device. Or tap an already-paired Bluetooth device on the list to make it the active one. Later, if you want to summon the device you just disconnected back into service, just tap its name in this list—you don't need to pair it again.

Advanced Phone Settings

You can further fine-tune thwe way your phone works by adjusting the following settings. To see them, open the Phone application, and then go to the application menu and tap Preferences. You'll see a screen with the following settings:

- **Phone Number.** No surprise here: This section of the screen displays the number people can use to call your Pre.

- **When Typing in Key Pad.** Normally, when you have the dial pad open but type in numbers from the keyboard, the Pre displays only numbers in the dial pad. If you turn on Show Contact Matches, the Pre displays both numbers and letters when you dial from the keyboard, and it automatically searches your Contacts list for matches.

- **Dialing.** The Pre usually plays a short tone when you type a number, no matter how long you press the key. When that's the case, you see the word "Short" in this section of the Phone Preferences screen. If you want the Pre to play longer tones (so the tone plays until you release the key), tap Short, and in the list that appears, tap Long. You might need this option to communicate with a computer that recognizes touch tones, like those irritating customer-service voice menus some companies use.

- **Dialing Shortcuts.** As discussed on page 83, these are shortcuts to the office prefixes you may dial at work.

- **Network.** As you know, your Pre uses Sprint's nationwide network. If you travel outside Sprint's calling area (you can check its rough boundaries on the map at *http://tinyurl.com/n4yoef*), Sprint hands off your call to a carrier that services that area, so your calls go through *that* company's network instead. This is known as *roaming* (because you "roam" away from your regular carrier). As of this writing, you don't have to pay extra to roam within the U.S. under Sprint's Pre wireless plans (see page 222), but travelling overseas is a whole different ball of wax, as you learned earlier in this chapter (page 84).

If Sprint does get around to charging for roaming and you want to keep costs down by exclusively using the Sprint network, go to this section of the Phone Preferences screen and tap Voice Network. In the list that pops up, tap Sprint Only. Now your Pre makes and accepts calls only when you're within Sprint's coverage area. If you change your mind, or need to make a call from outside Sprint's boundaries, simply change this setting back to Automatic.

This section of the screen also has a Data Roaming item. *Data roaming* refers to stuff you do besides place phone calls—browse the web, for example, or send or receive email. Turning on the Data Roaming setting lets you do these things even when you're outside Sprint's coverage area. To do that, tap Data Roaming, and in the list that appears, tap Enabled.

Note You can only turn data roaming on or off when you have the Voice Network option set to Automatic. If that option is set to Sprint Only, you won't even see the Data Roaming option.

- **Accessibility.** People who are deaf, hard of hearing, or have other language or speech barriers use TTY or TDD phones. You can use some of these devices with the Pre by plugging them into the headset jack. To use such a device, move the switch next to TTY/TDD on the Phone Preferences screen from Off to On. (Note that when you connect this kind of device, you disable the Pre's audio modes, including the ability to hold the phone up to your ear and hear callers.)

- **Network Settings.** From time to time, Sprint may update your phone. You'll receive notifications when updates are available. But if you want to manually check for updates, then tap Update Network Settings here.

- **Preferred Roaming List.** If you're taking the Pre outside your home service area and have to select a roaming carrier, tap Update PRL to get what Sprint considers your best possible service options. Contact Sprint with questions about how often you might want to update the list.

- **Voicemail Count Reset.** As noted earlier, sometimes the Pre is a little slow about setting your voicemail count back to zero. To do so manually, press this button.

What's My Number?

You call other people all the time, but you rarely call yourself, so you might just forget your own number. If you find yourself in that spot, don't worry. As explained in the previous section, you can find your number near the top of the Phone Preferences screen (to get there, open the Phone program, go to the application menu, and tap Preferences).

Another option is to go to the Launcher and tap the Device Info icon, which looks like a white letter *i* in a blue circle. The Device Information screen that appears displays your number right near the top.

Preferences ▼	2:51	🛜 ⬝⫯⫯ 🔋

ⓘ Device Information

NAME

Ed Baig's Pre ›

PHONE

PHONE NUMBER	
BATTERY	28%
MEMORY	8 GB
AVAILABLE	1.6 GB
VERSION	Palm webOS 1.0.2

Chapter
5

The Pre as Organizer

Y ou've got places to go, people to see, and things to do, and you need a way to stay on top of it all.

Palm has made gadgets to help you manage and organize daily tasks since its iconic Palm Pilot PDA (personal digital assistant) that came out in 1996. PDAs are now passé, but the organizational functions they provide—a calendar, to-do list, and memo program—are as essential as ever, and the Pre handles these tasks with panache.

This chapter focuses on the small things the Pre does that make a big difference in your too-busy life—its organizer features. You'll learn to schedule appointments for one-time and recurring events, create a to-do list with prioritized tasks, and write notes to jog your memory.

The Calendar

As a busy person, you probably use more than one calendar: A Microsoft Exchange calendar at work, a Google Calendar that reminds you about your kids' activities, and perhaps a third calendar for friends' events on Facebook. The Pre lets you look at all these events in one place, or view the calendars individually.

When you first launch the Calendar program, the Pre displays your consolidated calendars in a single view—the aptly named All Calendars view—and color-codes the events so you know which calendar they came from. You can choose an individual-calendar view by tapping "All" in the date banner, which displays a drop-down list of all your calendars. Tap the name of the calendar you want to see individually.

Whichever calendar you consult, you can display upcoming events by the day, week, or month.

Day, Week, and Month Views

When you first open the Calendar program (tap the Calendar icon in the Quick Launch panel), the Pre displays the current day broken into 1-hour timeslots. A *date banner* at the top of the screen displays the day of the week, date, and a pull-down menu listing all your linked calendars.

You can change the calendar view using the three icons at the bottom of the screen:

- **Tap the Day view icon** ▤ to see your appointments for a single day. If you don't have any appointments scheduled, all the time slots are available in 1-hour durations.

  As you add events, the Pre displays unscheduled periods of 90 minutes or longer using an "accordion" view: Rather than show lots of empty timeslots, it shows a scrunched-up section with a label on it that tells you how much unscheduled time that section represents. That way, you don't have to do as much scrolling to see all your commitments.

To expand the accordion to add an event, tap the duration label, and the calendar goes back to displaying 1-hour timeslots. Tap the duration label once more to recompress the view.

To go to the next or previous day, left- or right-swipe the touchscreen, respectively.

- **Tap the Week view icon** ▥ to see seven days of the calendar with scheduled appointments shaded in. The Pre circles the current day in blue.

  Left- or right-swipe to see the next or previous week. Tap on any one day to switch to Day view.

- **Tap the Month view icon**  . The Pre again displays events in shaded blocks and circles the current day in blue. Tap any day to open it in Day view. To go to the next or previous month, this time you swipe down or up (respectively).

Schedule Events

Your old paper calendar had nothing on the Pre (well, maybe your old Norman Rockwell calendar did). When it comes to making appointments and avoiding event conflicts, few calendars are as versatile or as easy to use as the Pre's calendar is.

As the next section explains, you can choose a calendar before you schedule an event. But here's a quick preview of your three main ways of scheduling appointments on the Pre:

- **By timeslot.** Tap the appropriate timeslot to schedule an event, and then enter the event's name—Sydney's soccer game, Lunch with the Big Cheese, whatever. This works great for scheduling events for today or in the next few days. The next page has details.

- **Specify a date.** Tap any timeslot, type in the event's name, and then tap the ⓘ icon to the right of the name to open a details page. Then tap the box near the top of the screen that shows the event's date and time, and use the scroll wheels on the page to select the event's date and start and end times. Page 110 has more about this method.

- **Jump to a specific date.** This is the best method when arranging an appointment well in the future. Open the application menu and tap Jump To, and then select the date you have in mind. See page 110 for the full scoop.

Choose a Calendar

Before you can schedule an event, you first have to decide which calendar you want to add the event to, the Pre calendar or one of your linked calendars. If you schedule an event while you're in the All Calendars view, the Pre records that event to your default calendar (see page 54). To add an event to another calendar, either the Pre's calendar itself or to one of your other (non-default) online calendars, choose the calendar by tapping "All" in the date banner and then tapping the name of the calendar you want to add the event to (the Pre's calendar is labeled "Palm Profile"). To get back to the All Calendars view, tap the calendar button in the upper-right part of the date banner, and then tap All Calendars.

> **Tip** If you don't like the colors the Pre assigns to your calendars, pick your own. Go to the Calendar program's application menu, tap Preferences & Accounts→Accounts, and choose a calendar (Palm Profile, Google, Facebook, or Exchange). Then tap the color assigned to this calendar to display a list of all your color choices. Tap the hue you want. This can be handy if you have more than one Google calendar in your account—one with U.S. holidays, say, and a friend's calendar you have permission to include with your own—because you can assign separate colors to each one.

Remember, if you schedule an event on the Pre's calendar, you can see that event only in the consolidated All Calendars view or in the Palm Profile calendar view—Synergy doesn't sync Palm Profile events with any of your online accounts.

> **Note** The Pre isn't compatible with iCal, the date book on Macs.

If you schedule an event in either the Google or Exchange calendar views, those events show up in the associated online calendars. (You can't schedule an event on the Facebook calendar on the Pre and have it appear in your online Facebook calendar because of restrictions imposed by the company.)

> **Note** Events you schedule in the All Calendars view automatically get assigned to your default calendar (see page 54).

Schedule an Event by Timeslot

Suppose your cousin unexpectedly comes to town and wants to meet for drinks after work. You're free at 6 p.m. so that's when you'll get together. The simplest way to schedule the event on your Pre is go into Day view (page 106) and tap on the 6 p.m. timeslot and type in *Drinks with Cuz*.

> **Note** The Pre automatically saves events when you use the back gesture (page 27) to close out of an event—you don't have to tap a Save or Done button.

This method works best for appointments you want to schedule for today, tomorrow, and perhaps the day or so after that. That's because it's a breeze to swipe left to skip ahead a few days, and then to tap the appropriate timeslot. As you move further into the future, however, you probably want to use one of the methods explained next.

Schedule a Future Event

If your event is days, weeks, months, or even *years* away, you can schedule an event in a couple of other ways.

Tap the Quick Launch panel's Calendar icon to open the calendar to the current day. Tap on any timeslot, enter the event's name, and then tap the ⓘ icon to the right of the event's name to open the calendar details page. (You can also enter the event's name on this page.) Now, tap the date-and-time box near the top of the page to set up the event. The Pre displays the current month, day, year, and start and end times in a set of tappable fields. Tap one and select a new time or date using the scrolling list that pops up. For example, to schedule an event for a different month, tap the current month and then scroll up or down to find the month you want and tap it. The scrolling list disappears, and the screen displays the month you selected. Repeat these steps for the day, year, and start and end times, and the Pre automatically saves the event.

Alternatively, when you open the Calendar, open the application menu and tap Jump To. The Pre displays the current month, day, and year in clickable windows. Select the event's date using the technique described above and then tap the Go To Date button. The calendar jumps to that date, where you can enter your event.

Tip You can also get to the Jump To screen by tapping the date banner at the top of any calendar view.

Return to the present

If you schedule an event months in the future and then want to return to the current date, open the application menu and tap Show Today or tap Jump To→Go To Today.

Change Event Durations

Back to grabbing that drink with your cousin. Out of the box, the Pre presumes that all your appointments will last an hour. So when you created the "Drinks with Cuz" event described above, the Pre automatically made the event 1 hour long. But your cousin knows how to knock back a few, and so do you, so your rendezvous will almost certainly last longer than an hour.

You change the length of an event in a couple of ways. First, you can change the Pre's default event duration from an hour to either 30 minutes or to 2 hours. To do that, go to the application menu and then tap Preferences & Accounts→Default Event Duration, and then tap either "30 minutes" or "2 hours".

But that option doesn't give you a whole lot of flexibility. What if a meeting is scheduled for an hour and a half? Or you're scheduling a convention that spans three days? In cases like these, you can't rely on the Default Event Duration setting—you have to manually tell the Pre how long the event will last.

To set the length of an appointment, do one of two things:

- If you haven't added the event to the calendar yet, tap the timeslot that reflects the starting time. The slot displays the words "New event" and an ⓘ icon. Tap the icon and follow the directions below.

- If you already scheduled the appointment, tap the event's name ("Drinks with Cuz" in the above example).

Either way, you see a screen that shows the event's details. In the cousin example, since you already tapped the 6 p.m. timeslot, Palm lists that as the event's start time. You can alter the start time, of course, if your plans change. But for now, you want to change the end time from 7 p.m. to something more realistic, like 9 p.m. or 10 p.m. Tap on the box that shows the event's date and time and, on the screen that appears, scroll down to the End section, and tap the hour box, which currently has a 7 in it.

A scrolling list appears. Scroll through the strip until you find the appropriate hour, and then tap it to lock in the new time. Tap other boxes to change the minutes or to change *PM* to *AM*. (You can change the day, month, and year as well, should your cousin postpone.)

Add a Location

If you tap the ① icon to set up an event or tap an event's name after you've added the event to your calendar, you can add a location to the event. Tap "Event location" on the screen that appears, and then type in the address.

Create a Recurring Event

The Pre assumes your events are one-time-only affairs unless you tell it otherwise. To set up a recurring event, tap the ⓘ in the appropriate timeslot or, for an existing appointment, tap the event's name; then tap No Repeat. On the list that appears, tap the appropriate button to repeat the event daily, weekly, or on weekdays. There's also a Custom option on the list, which lets you set up other schedules.

For example, things like birthdays and wedding anniversaries occur annually, but it'd be a drag to reenter these events every year. Rather than doing that, go to the festive date, then go to the application menu and tap New→Event. Then tap No Repeat→Custom→Daily→Yearly on [the date you selected]. Then make sure the box labeled "Forever" is checked (if it's not, simply tap it) so that the Pre schedules the event in perpetuity.

The Custom option also lets you set your own intervals for recurring events. If you tap Custom and then tap Daily, you can plug in the number of days between recurrences, from 0 to 99. So you can have an event that repeats every 9 days, say, or every 76 days.

The same principle applies to weekly events: You can use the Custom option to repeat an event every 1 to 99 weeks. You can also put a checkmark on the days within the weeks that you want an event to recur.

Set Reminders

You may be pretty good about checking your calendar, but nobody's perfect. The Pre can remind you about events to help jog your memory (but unless you change the Calendar program's settings, it doesn't create reminders automatically).

To add a reminder, tap the ⓘ after you select a timeslot for an event, or tap the name of an existing event. On the screen that appears, tap the words "No Reminder", and choose how far in advance you want the Pre to remind you. For events that last less than a day, you can choose to hear an alarm 5, 10, 15, or 30 minutes, 1 hour, or a day before the start time.

> **Note** Even for recurring events like birthdays, you can only set up a reminder for up to a day in advance, which isn't exactly a lot of time to pick a present and mail a card.

The Pre can deliver both audio and text reminders. The audio reminder is a single tone that stops a second later. To turn off this type of notification, go to the application menu and tap Preferences & Accounts. In the Event Reminders section of the screen that appears, tap the switch next to "Play sound" to change it from On to Off.

Note When you add a reminder to a repeating event, you see a screen asking whether you want to add the alarm to a single occurrence of that event (tap Change This Occurrence), or to the *entire* series (tap Change Series).

The text reminder, which shows up in the notification area at the bottom of the screen, always includes the name and time of the event. If you added a location to the event, that's listed, too. If the event is the result of a meeting request that came through Exchange (see page 116), you'll see an additional notification button, Contact Meeting Attendees. Tap it to send an email message to everyone who's coming to the meeting. Email automatically includes the attendees' addresses and adds "Running late, on my way…" to the message's body text, which you can change.

Tip If you miss a reminder (when you do, the large reminder notification becomes a tiny icon at the bottom of the screen) and want to see what it was for, go to the Calendar program's application menu and tap Missed Reminders (this option appears only when you've actually missed a reminder). Then scroll through the list of reminders, and tap Clear All when you've looked them over.

Reminder notifications include green Dismiss and yellow Snooze buttons. Tap Snooze to have the Pre remind you again in 5 minutes (you can't change the snooze interval), or Dismiss if you don't need any more nudging.

Add Notes

You may need a mental refresher to go along with any alarms you set for an event. To type one in, tap the name of an existing event, and near the bottom of the screen that appears, tap "Event notes". Then enter whatever you need to remember, from who's going to be joining you, to the purpose of the event. This info appears right under the event's title in Day view (page 106).

Schedule All-Day Events

Birthdays, anniversaries, and holidays eat up entire days, so there's no sense scheduling them for a specific timeslot. Fortunately, the Pre lets you schedule all-day events with a single tap. On the event duration screen, check the box next to the words "All day event".

If you already scheduled an event and find that it will end up taking the whole day, tap the event, then tap the date and time, and then check the "All day event" box. The Pre removes your original start and end times, and blocks out the whole day.

Respond to Meeting Requests

If a meeting request arrives on your Pre via the Email application, tap the request. Tap the green button in the body of the email to accept the invite, the red button to decline it, or the gray "?" button to think about it. Unless you outright decline, the Pre adds the event to your Exchange calendar.

If you open the Calendar program and tap on the event in your Exchange calendar, you'll see a box in the screen that pops up showing how many people plan on attending the meeting. Tap the number to see the name of the person who's organizing the meeting and of all the invitees, confirmed or not. If one of those folks is among your contacts, you can tap his name to bring up his contact card. If someone isn't a contact, tapping summons a card with an "Add to Contacts" option.

You may also receive a meeting request that originated in a Google calendar. If a request like this appears in your Gmail inbox, the invitation won't have the Accept or Decline buttons you see in Exchange requests. Instead, the message includes a link. Click the link to have the Pre open its web browser (page 160) and take you to a Google page where you respond. If you accept the request, it shows up in your Google calendar and, after a sync, on your Pre's consolidated calendar. You'll receive a reminder on the Pre at the appointed time.

Delete an Event

To delete a calendar entry, go to the event, open the application menu, and tap "Delete event"; then confirm your intentions by tapping Delete again. If it's a recurring event, you can delete just that instance (if you're out sick, say), or wipe out *all* instances of that event.

View Combined and Separate Calendars

Tip If you use a Google calendar online with Google Weather, Google Weather appears in the Pre's Calendar program, too.

The Pre displays all your calendars in a single, consolidated view—called, appropriately, All Calendars—and color-codes events so you know which event came from which calendar (see the Tip on page 110 to learn how to change those colors). You can look at the calendars individually, too: Tap the word "All" in the date banner, and in the list that appears, tap the name of the calendar you want to peruse.

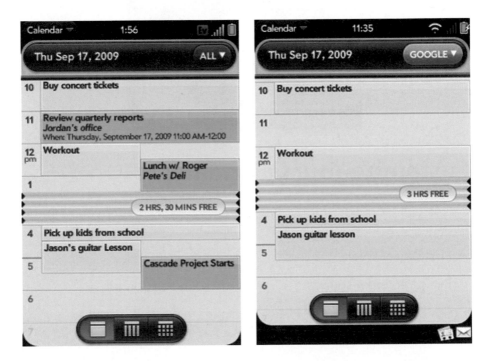

Tip The Pre's *peek* feature is a neat way to glance from the current screen to the previous or following screen without actually *going* there. For example, in the Calendar application, you can peek at the next day's appointments. To do so, place your finger in the middle of the screen, and drag it far enough to the left so that a portion of the next day's calendar slides into view. When you've seen what you need to see, drag the calendar back to today's view.

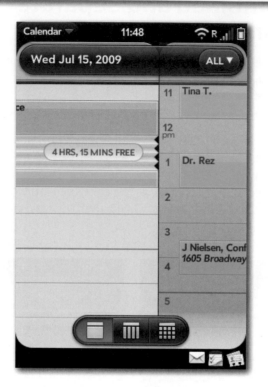

Customize Your Calendar

You have other options for making calendars your own, each found in the application menu under Preferences & Accounts:

- **First Day of Week.** Pick anything from Sunday to Monday.

- **Event reminder sounds.** You can have a sound play or not.

- **Day start and end.** If you don't work 9 to 5, choose another time span. (The Pre displays a slightly bolder line on your calendar at these start and end times. Consider them subtle reminders of when you should be at work.)

- **Default calendar.** This is the calendar an event gets assigned to if you create it in the All Calendars view. At first, the Pre automatically chooses Palm Profile as your default calendar, but when you sync a new calendar, that new one becomes the default. If you want to change the default calendar, tap this setting and then tap another calendar's name.

Tasks

Some busy people like to order their day by the tasks they need to complete. If you're a list person, the Task program has your name on it. It has more features than a simple to-do list: It lets you name lists, assign priorities to tasks, and check off tasks you complete. It also organizes your tasks into groups of related errands called *task lists,* described in the next section.

Tasks and Task Lists

You have to assign tasks to task lists, which are collections of related chores. So you could, for example, set up a task list called *Taxes* with list items for calling your accountant, collecting financial statements, and making donations.

When you open the Tasks application by tapping on its Launcher icon, you see a button labeled "List all tasks". That's the master list of *all* your tasks, culled from individual task lists.

Create a New Task List

To create your first to-do list, tap the Add Task List icon ✒, at the bottom of the Tasks program's main screen. That brings you to a fresh task list with your cursor in the List Name box. Type in a name (Household Chores, PTA, or whatever), and then tap the ✒ button to start adding tasks. Type in the name of the task where it says "Task name", and then press the Enter key ⏎ to finish entering that task and start writing a new one.

To put new tasks in an existing task list, from the main Tasks screen, tap a list's name to open it, and then tap the Add Task icon ✦.

Assign Priorities and Due Dates

If you have a long list of tasks but limited time, categorize tasks by priority. Tap the list's name to see the individual tasks, and then tap the ① to the right of a task. Tap the word "Normal" and choose low, normal, or high priority. When you do, Tasks color-codes that task by making the task's text gray (low priority), black (normal), or red (high).

From this screen, you can also change the list this task appears on. The list it currently belongs to is shown in a box next to the word "List". Tap this box to display the names of all the other task lists on your Pre, and then tap the name of the list you want to move the task to.

While you're here, you may want to set a due date for your task. Tap the words "No due date" (that's the Pre's default setting), and then tap the appropriate due date in the list that appears: today, tomorrow, one week from now, one month from now, or any other day you choose. After you do that, the due date appears next to the task's name. (The Pre calculates the date based on your selection, so if you choose "tomorrow", you see tomorrow's date.) You can also leave yourself notes about the task at hand by tapping in the area labeled Notes in the bottom half of the screen.

On the main Tasks screen, you'll see a number next to "List all tasks" and next to various other task lists. These numbers represent unfinished tasks that are due today or that are now past their due dates. Tap a number to see which tasks you have to tackle immediately. You'll also see a tiny notification icon about them in the bottom-right corner of the screen. Tap the icon to summon the notification dashboard, which also displays the number of outstanding tasks in an icon, right next to the name of the task that's the longest overdue. Tap the number to open the Tasks program, or tap the overdue task's name to jump to that specific task.

To set a single due date for all the tasks in a list, tap the list's name on the main Tasks screen, then open the application menu, and then tap "Set Due Dates For All...". On the screen that appears, pick the date you want.

Check Off Completed Tasks

To record a completed task, find the task, and then tap the box to its left to add a checkmark (and congratulate yourself on a task well done).

You can check off *all* the tasks in a list by opening the application menu and tapping Mark All→Mark All Completed. Or if you've been lax, choose Mark All Incomplete to removes the checkmarks beside every task to remind you that you've got lots of unfinished business.

To wipe completed tasks off a list, open the application menu and tap Purge Completed. You can also get rid of a task or task list (with or without uncompleted tasks) by swiping it off the side of the screen. To make sure you don't accidentally delete a task or list, you have to tap Delete to confirm your decision.

Memos

Memos are less structured than task lists—they're just notes to yourself. You can use the Pre's handsome Memos application—it looks like a mini-corkboard, complete with pushpins and a faux Post-it Notes pad—to jot down grocery lists or repairs you want your mechanic to make.

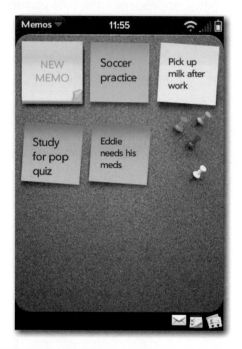

Tip If you sync your Outlook notes with the Pre through Microsoft Exchange ActiveSync, those notes appear on the Pre as Memos. Same goes for notes you import from Outlook via the Data Transfer Assistant described on page 70.

To create a memo, go to the Launcher and tap the [icon]. Then tap the New Memo box, which looks like a Post-it Note. Enter your note-to-self and you're done—the Pre automatically saves your memos.

Note You can tap and hold a memo to drag it to a different spot on the corkboard, but the Pre makes sure they all stay aligned in a grid.

You can edit a memo by tapping it, moving the cursor to any point in the text, and typing away. (Hold the orange button on the keyboard, and slide your finger on the screen to move the cursor.)

Tip Universal search (page 46) doesn't search Memos from Card view. But when you're in the Memos program itself, you can search memos by typing a term into the keyboard.

The Pre automatically colors each memo you write, making it yellow, green, blue, or pink. You can change the color to differentiate them—blue for notes about your kids and green for your spouse, for example. In the memos list, tap the memo in question to open it, then tap the page curl at the bottom-right corner of the screen. Then tap one of the colored squares that appear to select a color.

To throw away a memo you're done with, open the memo and then go to the application menu and tap Delete.

Chapter

6

The Pre as Message Center

SET UP YOUR EMAIL ACCOUNTS

Don't let just anybody know you've got a Palm Pre—unless you want to hear from them regularly. As you'll discover in this chapter, the Pre is a wickedly intelligent communications hub—in the way it handles email (fully formatted and complete with attachments), text and picture messages, and chat or instant messaging. Palm's Synergy has a hand in all this, too, in the way it brings these messages together.

The bad news? You can't use "I never got that email" as an excuse anymore.

Set Up Your Email Accounts

You probably already have a few different email addresses—one for work, one for personal stuff, and maybe one for the community group you volunteer for. The Pre can coordinate all these email accounts with no problem, whether they're web-based, such as Gmail, Hotmail, and Yahoo, or a Microsoft Exchange account issued to you by your employer. The exact process for setting up each account is slightly different, but this section explains everything you need to know. You can even set up a brand-new email account on your Pre if you like.

If you set up your Pre to sync with Google and Exchange accounts as described on page 58, you already have fully functioning Gmail and Exchange email accounts.

If you don't have a Gmail or Exchange account and haven't set up any other email accounts on the Pre, get started by tapping the Email icon ✉ on the Quick Launch panel. You'll see the Add An Account screen below. Type your email address and password in the spaces provided, and then tap the Sign In button.

> **Tip** You can summon the Add An Account screen anytime, since you likely have several personal and work email accounts. Open the Email application, go into the application menu, and tap Preferences & Accounts→"Add an Account" (you may have to scroll down the screen to see this option).

What happens next depends on the account you're trying to add. With most popular email services, like AOL, EarthLink, Hotmail, and Yahoo, all you have to do is type in your email address and password, and then tap the Sign In button. Then you wait a half-minute or so while a circle spins to the right of a dark-gray Sign In button. That's your clue that the Pre is adding the account; shortly thereafter the button turns a lighter gray and changes to read "Signing In". If everything goes according to plan, this latest email account appears on a screen with all your other accounts. From there, you're good to go: You can start sending and reading emails as described later in this chapter (see page 133).

Tip Filling in user names and passwords to set up popular email accounts such as AOL and Hotmail is supposed to work smoothly, but that's not always the case. If you run into a snag, try this: Turn off the Pre's WiFi connection by tapping the connection menu in the right-hand corner of the status bar; then try setting up email again. If that doesn't work, contact Sprint or your email provider.

You may need to provide more information to set up some email services. After the circle stops spinning, you might see spaces for the following info, some of which you may not know (you have to enter this stuff by hand, but some of it may already be filled in):

- **Account type.** Your choices are POP or IMAP. The main distinction between the two is that with an IMAP account, you get the same view of your mail—messages received, sent, and saved—from any PC, whether it's your Pre, a laptop at home, or a desktop at work. With a POP account, your email account may look different from PC to PC, including your Pre. Here's more about these accounts:

    - *POP* (Post Office Protocol; sometimes called POP3). POP accounts download new email messages to whatever PC you access your account with. If you check your messages with your Pre, for example, those messages download to your Pre, they don't stay on your email service's giant, centralized computer (called a *server*). If you go home, start up your laptop, and want to reply to a message you read while on your Pre, you're out of luck—that message now resides on your Pre. POP accounts don't act as a central hub for email.

    To compensate for fractured email accounts, many POP services let you leave a copy of your incoming and sent mail on their server, so you can access them from any computer (including your Pre). But other changes you make to mail—if you start the draft of a message, for example--won't be reflected on the server, which means you can still experience disjointed email accounts, the main drawback of POP services.

— *IMAP* (Internet Mail Access Protocol) is the more modern type of email account. It also stores your email on servers, but it synchronize changes you make to your email account across all your PCs. Thus you have a consistent view of your email, no matter what PC you use to access it, including your Pre.

The downside to IMAP accounts, especially ones with strict storage limits, is that you have to delete messages you've read so you don't run out of storage space.

Bottom line: If you have a choice between IMAP or POP on a given account, choose IMAP.

- **A potpourri of geeky settings.** These settings include incoming and outgoing mail server names, port numbers, and "SSL requirements," a type of email security. Don't worry—you don't have to know this stuff off the top of your head, or even know what it means. To figure out what to fill in here, contact your ISP (Internet service provider), or the company or school that set up your account.

Microsoft Exchange Accounts

The folks at Palm know that Microsoft Exchange is the most common type of email account companies give employees, so your Pre is meant to work with Exchange right out of the box.

The drill for setting up Exchange mail is similar to the process described in the previous section: Tap the Email icon in the Quick Launch panel, and type in your user name and password. Then, when the "Signing In" circle stops spinning, tap the POP box, and instead of choosing POP or IMAP as the Mail Type, select Exchange (EAS—the AS part stands for ActiveSync). After all that, fill in the web address (something like *webmail.yourcompany.com*), domain (typically your company's name with no spaces), user name (whatever appears before the @ in your email address), and password in the boxes provided. When you're done, tap Sign In.

If you need help with any of this setup, talk to someone in your company's IT department.

Customize Your Accounts

You can do a few more things to get your email accounts just the way you want them. (If you're dying to send email, you can come back to this section later; see page 133 to learn how to write messages.) In Email's application menu, choose Preferences & Accounts, and then tap the name of the account you want to tweak. You'll see the following settings:

- **Account Name.** Unless you change this setting, your accounts will be called things like AOL, Hotmail, Yahoo, and so on. But you can call them Janie's AOL, Lyle's Hotmail, Sandy's Yahoo, or whatever you like. Just tap on Account Name and type the new name over the old one.

- **Full Name.** This is the name people will see when you send mail, so decide whether to go formal (Robert) or not (Bobby).

- **Show Notification.** Slide this switch to the On position to see a notification at the bottom of the screen every time a new email message arrives in your inbox. These alerts are supposed to be unobtrusive, but if you get a lot of email, you may want to leave this option turned off so you don't get distracted every few seconds.

- **Play Sound.** If you're on the edge of your seat waiting for important email, you can tell the Pre to play a clang noise every time messages arrive. Just remember that this sound may drive the people around you nuts—especially if you're in a movie theater or office. You can silence these sounds by turning the ringer switch off.

- **Vibrate.** This option, which appears only if the Play Sound setting is turned off, is a more discreet way to learn of incoming email. It's not totally silent, but it's less likely to annoy other people.

- **Signature.** This is a snippet of text that goes at the bottom of every message you send. The default here is "Sent from my Pre", but you can change that to your contact info, favorite quote, or whatever. You can turn off signatures altogether by tapping the account name, tapping the signature box, and then deleting the text that's in the box.

- **Reply-to Address.** If you want people to see and reply to an email address other than the one you sent the message from, type that address here. This can be handy when you want to keep a personal email address private.

- **Sync deleted mails.** This setting is for POP accounts only. If you flip this switch on, your email will get deleted from the server when you delete it on the Pre. If you think you'll check this email account from another machine, like a home PC, leave the setting off.

- **Show Email.** Choose whether you want to retrieve 1 day's worth of mail, 3 days', 7 days', 2 weeks', 1 month's, or *all* the mail in your inbox. Your choice here depends on how much email you get—if you get tons of email each day, "1 day" is a good pick.

- **Get Email.** Here's where you tell the Pre how often you want it to fetch mail. If your email service can *push* mail so that it arrives seconds after someone sends it, you can set this to "As items arrive" so they show up in real time, just as if you were at a desktop PC.

  The downside to fetching mail right away is that it drains the Pre's battery much more quickly. If that's a problem, choose a different interval: options range from 5 minutes to 24 hours. Or select Manual to check mail only when you have time to read it.

- **Default Folders.** You only see this setting for IMAP accounts like AOL, Gmail, or Yahoo. You get to specify the folders where the program puts sent mail, drafts, and trash, depending on your email program. You'll set up such folders (if you set them up at all) on a desktop or laptop computer, not on your Pre. (Folders are what email accounts use to organize your messages; you typically have folders for things like sent messages, drafts, and so on.)

Close an Account

If you change jobs, schools, or just want to stop using an email account that seems to get nothing but spam, it's easy to make a clean break. Go to the application menu, tap Preferences & Accounts, tap the name of the account that's getting the heave-ho, and then tap the red Remove Email Account button. If you tap the button by accident or have second thoughts, just tap Keep Email Account.

> **Note** When you close an email account, all that account's messages get deleted, too.

Edit Account Info

Sometimes you need to change your user name, password, or other settings. For example, your company might make you change your password regularly for security reasons. To make such changes, go to Email's application menu, tap Preferences & Accounts, and then tap the name of the account you want to edit. Tap the Change Login Settings button and make your changes.

Merge Accounts

Through Palm Synergy (see page 54), your Pre merges all your email messages into one inbox. Palm figures that if all the messages are meant for you anyway, why should you have to search around in several accounts to find a piece of mail?

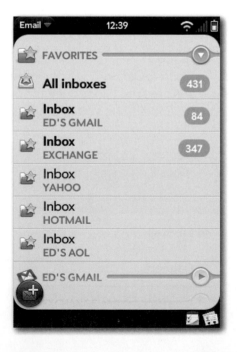

Here's a cool feature. Even though all the messages end up in the same inbox, the Pre remembers which email address each one was sent to. So when you reply to a message, the recipient sees the same From address they sent the original email to—that way, you won't confuse people by responding from a different email address. And if you send a new message (in other words, one that's not a response to anything) from this inbox, it goes out via the designated default account you learned to set up on page 57.

But a merged view can have the opposite effect, too—if you get gobs of mail by consolidating accounts, it can be overwhelming. So Palm lets you view accounts individually, too.

When you first open Email, you see a Favorites folder, which the Pre sets up automatically. The Favorites folder is already open (you can tell by the downward-pointing arrow) and it contains your consolidated inbox ("All Inboxes") listed first and, below that, inboxes for each of your linked email accounts ("Inbox: Ed's Gmail", for example; see the figure on page 137).

For now, close the Favorites folder by tapping the down arrow so you can see how the Pre organizes your *individual* email accounts.

Normally, the Email program organizes individual accounts so that that account's inbox appears right under the account name ("Exchange", for example). Then it displays any subfolders you set up in the inbox, followed by your outbox and then any other folders in the account (for deleted mail, drafts, sent mail, and so on).

If you open a particular mail folder frequently, you can make it easy to get to by adding it to the Favorites folder (see next page for instructions on how to do so).

All Inboxes is one of two *smart folders* in Email (the other is All Flagged, covered on page 143). If you don't see this folder, open the application menu and tap Preferences & Accounts, and flip the switch under Smart Folders to turn on All Inboxes.

Make a folder a favorite

As noted above, your favorite mail folders sit inside the Favorites folder the Pre has set up, which is at the top of the list showing all your email accounts and folders. To add a folder to Favorites, tap the star ☆ to the right of the folder's name.

Reorder your email accounts

You can change the order in which the individual accounts appear in the account list. Go to the application menu and tap Preferences & Accounts, and then tap and hold an account's name and drag it up or down in the list. When it's where you want it, lift your finger off the screen.

> **Note** When a folder is open, if you tap its name at the top of the screen, you see the time of your last sync (page 54 covers syncing your Pre), when the next sync is scheduled, and the total number of emails in that folder.

Composing Messages

Now that your account is set up just so, you're ready to write your first message. (Send this maiden missive to somebody really important.)

Here's how to send an email on the Pre:

❶ **If you're not already in Email, tap the Email icon in the Quick Launch panel.**

❷ **Tap the ✉ icon in the bottom-left corner of the screen.** The window showing your email folders shrinks and is ushered into Card view, while a new card for sending email slides into view and takes over your screen.

❸ **If you want to send the message from an account other than your default account (see Chapter 3), tap the From box to change the outgoing address.** (If you have only one account, you can skip this step.) When you tap From, a list drops down showing all the accounts you can send mail from.

❹ **Use the keyboard to type in the recipient's email address.** This is the slowest option. Fortunately, there's a better way: Use your Contacts list. Type a few letters of your friend's first, last, or company name, or his initials, and the Pre guesses who you mean by displaying a list of possibilities. Keep typing until you narrow down the list. Tap on a name to select that person.

Another option is to tap the Contacts icon ⬛ in the To box to see all your contacts. Scroll up or down the list until you find the right person, and then tap his name. If he has more than one email address, tap the one you want.

Tip If you make a mistake and tap the wrong contact to add as your recipient, press and hold your finger on the person's name in the To box. When you lift your finger, the Pre highlights the name in yellow. Press backspace ⬅ on the keyboard to wipe out the name so you can substitute a new one, or tap the To box so your cursor appears just after the recipient's name, and then press backspace.

❺ **If you want to send a message to more than one person, start typing a new name in the To box, or tap the ⬛ icon and add more people as explained in step 4.** If you tap directly on the word "To"—there's a little button there—options appear so you can add recipients in dedicated Cc and Bcc boxes.

As you probably know, *Cc* stands for *carbon copy.* When you put someone's address in this field, it's like an FYI to that person—you're keeping him in the loop, but don't expect a response.

Bcc stands for *blind carbon copy.* Use this field to keep people in the loop while keeping their names and addresses from the person in the To field. Whether you use this field for good or evil is up to you.

⑥ If you like, enter a subject for your email by tapping in the space provided. This is optional, but sending emails without subjects is considered poor form.

⑦ Set a priority. Again, this is optional. An email's *priority* tells the recipient how urgent it is. If you don't set a priority, the Pre assumes the message is Normal Priority—nothing special. But if your message is super-urgent, go to the application menu and tap High Priority. When you do, the horizontal line under the message's subject changes from blue to red. If you decide before sending the message that it doesn't deserve special status after all, go to the application menu again and tap Normal Priority.

Tip Don't use the High Priority label for all your emails—if you do, people will ignore your messages even when they really are urgent.

⑧ Type the text of your message. Finally, the most important step of all: jotting down your brilliant thoughts. Simply tap in the big blank area in the lower part of the screen and type away. If you want to emphasize certain points in your email, press Sym+B on the keyboard (that's the Sym and B keys simultaneously) to add bold type to the text **like this** or Sym+I to italicize it *like this.* You can either hold these keyboard combinations down before you start typing text, or highlight text you've already typed (as explained on page 54), and then apply the bolding or italics. To go back to typing regular text, just press the Sym+B or Sym+I combination again.

⑨ Tap ✐ to send your message. Your message wings its way through cyberspace.

Add Attachments

When you send an email, you may want to send more than just text. You can attach documents, pictures, videos, and music files.

To add an attachment when writing a message, tap the paperclip button 📎 in the bottom-left corner of the screen.

The Pre assumes you want to attach an image file, so it displays all the picture folders on your Pre. If you do want to send a picture, tap the folder where it lives, and then tap the picture. Finally, tap the Attach Photo button at the top of the screen.

If you want to send some other kind of file, tap one of the other icons at the bottom of the screen. From left to right (after the pictures icon), they represent videos, music files, and documents. When you tap the appropriate icon, the Pre displays only files of that type. Tap a file to attach it.

Note You can attach more than one file to an email. But your ISP, employer, or the company that hosts your email account probably limits how much memory the files can take up. These restrictions are a two-way street—the person you're sending the email to may also have limits on what size files he can receive.

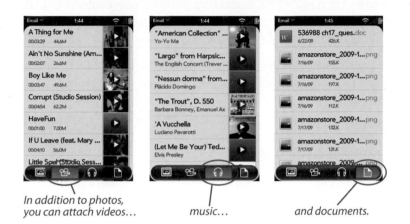

In addition to photos, you can attach videos…   *music…*   *and documents.*

Tip You can take a photo to email to someone from within the Email application. To do that, tap the paperclip button in the lower left of your screen. By default, that brings up the image file screen, which, in addition to listing existing photos, has a button for taking a photo on the fly, "New Photo." Tap it and the Pre opens the Camera application. For more on taking pictures on the Pre, turn to page 204.

Read Your Mail

Sending email is only half the fun. You want to check out what people send to you, too.

Owning a Pre is like having a mailroom in your pocket: It fetches and sorts email however you like (see page 129 for details on setting your preferences).

Pushed emails (see page 131) show up on your Pre as soon as they're sent, and other messages show up according to the polling schedule you set up, as explained on page 131. Depending on how you customized your email accounts (as explained on page 129), you can find out when messages show up either through the notification dashboard (see page 49), a sound, or both.

Getting mail is easy. The Pre syncs your email accounts any time you open a mail folder by tapping it. Assuming you set up your accounts as described earlier in this chapter (see page 126), when you open the Email application, you see a list of your accounts. If you don't see all the folders in an account, tap the arrows next to each account name (or Favorites) to bring all the folders out of hiding.

To retrieve messages, tap the name of the inbox you want to check, and then tap a message to open it.

If you've already opened a message, you can hop to the next or previous message in that folder by tapping the left- or right-pointing arrow in the message's subject line. To check mail for another account, use the back gesture (see page 27) to return to the account list.

When you're reading a message, you can use some of those nifty finger gestures you learned earlier (see page 29). To enlarge the text, for example, pinch your fingers out (though this might mean you have to pan around the screen to see the whole message).

The following sections cover all the things you can do once you open an email.

Reply or Reply All

To respond to an email, tap Reply 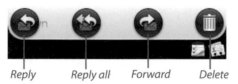. When you do, the Pre creates a new outgoing message with the From box already filled in with your email address and the To box filled in with the sender's name. The text of the original message appears in the body of the new message, with space above it for you to record your brilliant thoughts.

Reply   Reply all   Forward   Delete

If you tap Reply All 📭 instead, your response goes to the sender *and* everyone else who got the original.

> **Tip** You can't cut or copy text from an incoming email. But if you tap Reply, you can select text from the body of the original message, which has been copied into your reply, and then paste that text into another message or application. If you forward a message as explained next, you *can't* cut or copy text this way.

Forward

When a message is so interesting, important, or silly that you want to share it with all your friends, tap Forward 📧. The Pre creates a new message with room at the top for you to add your own two cents, and a subject line that reads "Fw: [Original Subject Line]".

> **Tip** If you have a Microsoft Exchange email account (see page 129), you may get meeting invitations in your inbox. To open an invite, just tap it; then tap again to accept, decline, or tentatively accept it. If you accept (or tentatively accept), the event appears on your calendar (see page 105). You can reply to or forward such invites just like any other email, but you *can't* invite others to a meeting through the Pre. If the event organizer cancels the meeting, you'll receive another email with a button that says, "Remove from Calendar".

Add Sender to Contacts

If you think you'll write a lot of emails to a person who's sent you a message, you can add her to your Contacts list—and the same goes for anyone in the Cc or Bcc line. To do that, tap the person's name or email address, and then tap the Add To Contacts button that appears. If it's a brand-new contact, tap Save As New. If you're adding new info to someone who's already one of your Contacts, tap Add To Existing, and then tap the name of the person you're updating.

Delete It

To get rid of a message you've read or (in the case of spam) have no intention of reading, tap the trash can button 🗑. (Hint: If the subject line promises you money or a job, it's probably spam.)

Don't fret if you tap the 🗑 button by accident and delete a message—it's not gone forever. Trashing a message just sends it to a Deleted Items folder, which is like death row for emails—they're not dead yet, but they're on the way. To pardon a message and bring it back to the land of the living, open the Deleted Items folder by tapping it in the account's folder list. Then just move the message back to the inbox or another folder as described in the next section.

To delete a message for good, you have to delete it from the Deleted Items folder, or whatever folder the account uses as the trash. Open the message within that folder (whatever it's called) and then tap 🗑.

You can also delete mail without opening it. From the inbox, flick the message either left or right off the edge of the screen.

Organize Your Messages

You can file email messages in different folders so your inbox doesn't get too "ginormous." To do that, open a message, and then go to the application menu. Tap "Move to Folder", and then tap the name of the folder you want to stash the message in. You can also mark messages in various ways, as the next couple of sections explain.

Mark a message as read or unread

Before you read a message, the Pre displays the sender's name in bold type. Once you open that email, the person's name appears in regular type. But you can mark it as unread so that the sender's name is bolded again. When you have the message open, head to the application menu and tap Mark As Unread. The opposite works, too: You can tap Mark As Read to not have the message appear in bold type.

Marking messages as unread can help remind you to deal with the message later on. Another option is to flag the message for follow-up.

Flag messages

If you don't have time to handle an email now, flag it so you'll remember to get back to it when you've got more time. To do that, open a message and then, in the application menu, tap Set Flag. Now, in your inbox, you'll see a little flag to the left of that message. To unflag a message, tap Clear Flag from the application menu.

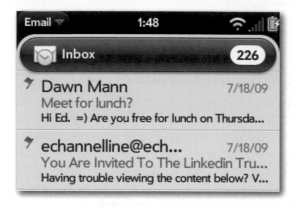

If you want to put all your flagged messages in one spot, you're in luck: Palm created a special smart folder (see page 129) that gathers those messages. To use it, go to the application menu, tap Preferences & Accounts, and flick the onscreen switch to turn on All Flagged. From now on, whenever you flag a message, it lands in the All Flagged folder, which is within the Favorites folder.

View message details

At just over 3 inches, the Pre's screen is pretty big for a cellphone, but still tiny compared with a standard computer monitor. Because screen space is a scarce resource, the Pre automatically hides basic info like the sender's—and any other recipient's—email address. To see a person's address, tap his name; if he's in your Contacts (see page 61), you'll see his phone number, too.

Open Attachments

You already know how to add attachments to messages. Here's how you fetch the attachments others send you.

If you see a paperclip next to a sender's name in the inbox, you know the email includes an attachment. When you open the message, the attachment's name appears in a bar just below the subject line, along with a number showing how big the file is.

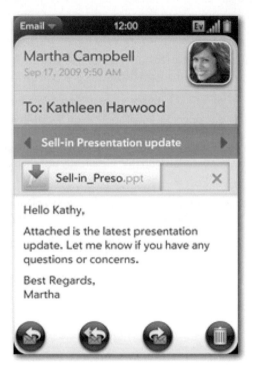

Tap the attachment to open it, or if it's a really big file, to start downloading it. If the Pre starts downloading a large file, the bar turns into a progress bar that shows you how the download's coming along.

If an email contains more than one attachment, when you open the message, you see the paperclip icon coupled with a circled number. That number tells you how many attachments came with the message. To open or download one of the attachments, tap this icon so that the Pre displays a list of all the attachments (along with their file sizes). Tap an attachment to open or download it.

If you downloaded a picture file, tap Copy To Photos to save it on your Pre. To view the image, open the Photos application (see page 207).

Microsoft Word documents that you download land in the Doc View application, which opens automatically when you tap the attachment. (To open the file again later, tap the Doc View icon in the Launcher.) Adobe PDF files go the appropriately named PDF View application, which you can also open later from the Launcher. To save these files, open the application menu in Doc View or PDF View, and then tap Save As. You can't edit the file names or the files themselves—you can only open the files and look at them.

If you tap an attachment and the Pre can't open it, you'll see a message telling you that the Pre doesn't support that type of file. Unfortunately, you're out of luck on the Pre. Try opening the attachment on a computer.

Tip You don't always have to open the Email application *directly* to send an attachment. If you open a Word document in Doc View or a PDF document in PDF View, you can go to the program's application menus and tap Share instead. This opens the Email application with that file already attached to a new email message.

In the Photos program application menu, you can send a picture through email or MMS (page 147) by tapping "Share via email" or "Share via MMS".

And you can share web pages in the Web application by opening the application menu and tapping Page→Share, which also opens Email.

Conversations

If you're under 30, you might think of email as passé and be more likely to send text messages from your phone. *Texting,* as it's called, means using the Short Messaging Service, better known as *SMS.* Text messages are limited to 160 characters max (about two relatively lengthy sentences, including spaces and punctuation). If you send text to an email address as noted below, the characters in the address count against the 160-character limit.

Text messages have a lot in common with email. The messages go out right away, and the recipient doesn't have to act on them immediately (they're waiting for him until he has time to respond), and text messages don't interrupt what people are doing. In fact, you can send or receive text messages even when you're on the phone. A good way to do this is to switch the call to speakerphone (see page 91) or a headset (see page 97) to free up your hand for typing.

The Pre can also send picture messages through MMS (Multimedia Messaging Service), but not video (though it can *play* video attachments received as part of an MMS). And as of this writing, Sprint's Pre service plan includes all forms of messaging.

Synergy gathers all the messages on a single topic into a single conversation or *thread.* Conversations can include text messages, multimedia files, and instant messaging (IM) communications (see page 148).

You can carry on multiple exchanges on a single topic and, at the same time, have several of these separate conversations going on at once.

As you have conversations, all the messages sent back and forth between you and the other person appear in the upper part of the screen, and you type your messages in the lower part

The Messaging screen has two tabs at the top: Tap the Conversations tab to see all text and MMS exchanges, or tap the Buddy List tab to see your IM buddies as described on page 149.

Texting

To start a conversation, tap the Messaging icon 💬 in the Launcher to open the Messaging application, and then:

❶ **Tap the ⟳ icon to send a new message.**

❷ **Tap the To box and enter the first or last name of a contact, a screen name, phone number, or email address, or tap the 🔳 to open your Contacts list.** Just as with email, you can add multiple recipients.

❸ **Enter the message text in the space at the bottom of the screen.** Remember, you only have 160 characters to express yourself. So use shortcuts like *r*, instead of *are*, or *2nite* instead of *tonight*. Once you reach the limit, the Pre won't let you add any more characters. Instead, it automatically starts a second text message to the same recipient, so you can get your complete message across.

❹ **Tap ✐ to send your message.** You'll see your outgoing message in a conversation area like the one shown below. When the person responds, his chatter gets added to the screen.

Send Picture Messages

The procedure for sending multimedia messages is almost the same as for sending text messages. To send an MMS, open the Messaging application, and then tap the 𝒪 button to bring up a list of all your picture folders. Tap the folder that holds the picture you want to add to your message and tap that photo. Or tap New Photo to snap a new image. Then tap Attach Photo, and add any text you want to send along with the image. Follow steps 3 and 4 of the previous section to send the picture along with the text.

If you've already started typing text and want to add a picture, open the application menu and then tap Add Picture.

Note Pictures you send via MMS have to be in the JPG format, and the files have to be smaller than 600KB. If they're not, the Pre automatically converts them to the proper format and resolution. Also, keep in mind that, in the United States anyway, relatively few phones can receive pictures sent by way of MMS. If the recipient's phone can't get the MMS, a message will be sent back to your Pre saying that the delivery failed.

If a friend sends you a picture through MMS, you see the image right in the message. To save it, tap Copy Photo, and the Pre saves it in the Messaging folder inside the Photos application.

Note You can't *send* video on your Pre using MMS, but if someone attaches a video to an MMS they send you, you can watch it by opening the Pre's Videos application (see page 20).

Advanced Messaging Tricks

Here's more of what you can do with text and picture messages:

- **Add the sender to your Contacts list.** As with an email, you can add the person to your Contacts list or add more info to an existing contact. When you receive a message, simply tap the header and then tap Add To Contacts.

- **View Contacts information.** Tap a message's header to peek at that person's Contacts entry.

- **Dial a number.** If the message contains a phone number, simply tap the number to call it. Keep in mind that calls have a way of interrupting people in a way that text messages don't, so it's best to call only when the person explicitly asks you to.

Delete Messages and Conversations

You can drag individual messages or entire conversations off the side of the screen when you're done with them. When the Pre asks you to confirm your decision, tap Delete.

Chat in Real Time

As this book went to press, the Pre can work with chat or instant messaging (IM) applications from AIM (AOL Instant Messenger) and Google Talk, but not yet from other popular chat programs such as Yahoo Messenger or MSN Messenger.

Chatting via an IM application on the Pre is different from texting in that the conversation is immediate, just as if you were on the phone, except that you're typing instead of speaking. And unlike texting, there's no limit to the number of characters you can type.

If you already have an AIM or Google Talk account, you just need to set them up to work on your Pre. (If you don't have such an account but want one, go to *www.aim.com* or *www.google.com/talk*.) To do that, open the Messaging application by tapping its icon in the Launcher. When you add IM accounts, all your instant messaging contacts get added to Contacts. If a person is already in your contacts list, her IM address gets added to her profile page.

If this is the first time you opened the Messaging application, you'll see the Add An Account screen. Any other time, open the application menu and tap Preferences & Accounts→Add IM Account. Tap the button for either AIM or Google (depending on which one you want to add), enter your user name and password, and then tap Sign In.

Note To delete an IM account, go to the application menu and tap Preferences & Accounts, and then tap the account you want to remove. Finally, tap Remove Account. To delete an account, you have to be logged out of the account—if your name appears with a green dot beside it, the Remove Account option will be grayed out.

To start chatting with a friend inside Messaging, tap the Buddies button at the top of the screen instead of the Conversations button. You'll see a list of your friends, complete with a picture if they've added one.

Your Buddies list includes different-colored dots next to peoples' screen names that indicate whether people are free to chat. Available buddies have a green dot by their names. Buddies who are online but not available to chat—perhaps they stepped away from their computers—have an orange circle next to their names, and possibly details about their status ("be right back"). And offline buddies have gray circles.

Note You can indicate your own status by tapping the Buddies icon, then tapping the button in a bar at the very top of the screen, and finally tapping Available (to make the button turn green), Busy (orange), or "Sign off" (gray). In that same bar, you can type in a status message, like "Available, but only in a pinch" or "Out to lunch" so people know what you're up to. Your buddies can leave similar status messages.

Tip You can have the Pre display all your buddies or only those who are online (it automatically lists all your buddies unless you tell it otherwise). To switch from one option to the other, tap the application menu, and then tap either Show Offline Buddies or Hide Offline Buddies.

To start a conversation, tap the name of an available buddy, start typing in the box at the bottom of the screen, and then tap ⊲ to start the dialogue. If you want to chat with someone who's not on your Buddies list, tap ✪ from either the Buddies or Conversations view (depending on which button you pressed at the top of the screen), enter the person's screen name, or scroll through Contacts by tapping ⊟ to find their AIM or Google listing. Then type a message, cross your fingers, and hope that the person types back.

If you've already chatted with someone, from Conversations view, tap the existing conversation to resume where you left off.

When someone tries chatting with you, the Pre can alert you through the notification dashboard, by a sound, or both. To tell the Pre what you want it to do, go to the application menu, choose Preferences & Accounts, and tweak the notification settings.

Now that you know about all the different ways people can get in touch with you on the Pre, you can see that it's getting awfully hard to hide.

Chapter

7

The Pre as Web Browser

The technology that lets you bop around the Internet on handheld gadgets like the Pre has come a long way in the past couple of years. Cellphones made in 2007 and earlier let you *sort of* browse the Web, but what you typically saw were stripped-down versions of websites that came to be known as the "mobile Internet." Connections were poky on such devices, and you had trouble seeing graphics—if you got them at all. And you had to use funky text menus to get around online, so surfing wasn't even remotely like what you were used to on a desktop computer.

As you'll discover in this chapter, your Pre is light-years ahead of that. Web pages on the Pre look like they do on a desktop PC. First, you'll learn how to get your Pre connected to the Internet, then you'll hear about all kinds of neat things you can do online.

How the Pre Gets Online

Obviously, it'd be silly if you had to plug a wire into your Pre to connect it to the Internet—that would defeat the purpose of having a mobile gadget. So the Pre uses wireless networks to get online, and it connects wirelessly in three different ways. The method you choose determines how quickly websites will load. Of course, if you're somewhere with only one kind of network, you have to use whatever's available. The following sections explain your options, starting with the cellular networks that the Pre starts you out with by default, and then moving on to WiFi.

Sprint Mobile Broadband

It's a good thing geeks don't market products, because they come up with some wacky names for stuff, like calling certain kinds of wireless networks *EvDo* or *1xRTT,* which don't exactly roll off your tongue. Fortunately, the folks at Sprint have given the *EvDo* network (which stands for Evolution-Data Optimized or Evolution-Data Only) a more palatable moniker: Sprint Mobile Broadband.

Sprint Mobile Broadband is the fastest *cellular*, or traditional wireless *phone*, network on your Pre. The technology behind this network is known as *3G* (short for "third-generation"), a high-speed way of transmitting voice and data. It's the network you want to be on if you don't have access to a speedier WiFi network (covered in the next section). Sprint has been expanding this network for the past few years, but as the map below shows, 3G still isn't everywhere, especially in rural areas.

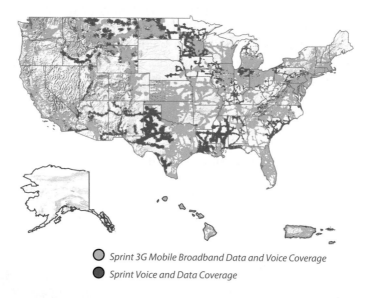

○ *Sprint 3G Mobile Broadband Data and Voice Coverage*
● *Sprint Voice and Data Coverage*

If you see the **Ev** icon on the upper-right corner of your Pre's screen—there's that EvDo thing again—you know you're connected to the 3G network and are probably humming along at a pretty good pace. That is, web pages materialize in a hurry.

If, on the other hand, you find you can grab a cup of coffee in the time it takes a web page to load, you're likely not on the 3G network. Take a gander at the upper-right corner of the screen: If it shows **1x**, you're on Sprint's *way* slower 1xRTT network (you don't even want to know what that stands for), yesterday's technology, which the phone will revert to when 3G isn't available.

The drawback to using either a 3G or 1xRTT is that you can't surf the Web while talking on the phone. WiFi connections, explained next, let you do both at the same time, and they're faster.

Wireless Hotspots

WiFi, another technology you can use to get online, is the zippiest way onto the Net with the Pre. To use this kind of connection, you have to tweak a couple of settings and be within a wireless *hotspot.* That's the area around the device that sends out a wireless network signal—it's usually a circle with about a 300-foot radius. You can find hotspots in plenty of places: airports, coffeehouses, libraries, schools, offices, parks, and lots of homes.

> **Tip** To see a list of hotspots near you, go to *www.jiwire.com* and in the Wi-Fi Users section, click the Wi-Fi Finder link; then type in your Zip code.

You'll hear other names for WiFi: Apple calls it AirPort and geeks call it *802.11* (pronounced "eight oh two dot eleven"). Technically, the Pre can use two kinds of WiFi networks: 802.11*b* and 802.11*g*—the letter on the end indicates how fast the network is and how far it reaches (they have the same range, but *g* is faster). All you need to know is that the Pre can connect to most common WiFi networks.

Out of the box, your Pre can't connect to WiFi networks, but that's easy to fix. Simply tap the network menu in the upper-right corner of the status bar, and then tap Wi-Fi→"Turn on Wi-Fi". You can close the connection later by tapping "Turn off Wi-Fi" instead.

You'll run into two types of WiFi networks:

- **Open networks.** These are open to anybody—you don't need a password. But resist the temptation to hop onto just any open hotspot: Some public hotspots are a haven for hackers. So if you use one, be extra careful about typing in passwords for banking and financial sites, as a hacker might be able to eavesdrop on your signal and get hold of them.

> **Note** Just because a network is open doesn't mean it's free. When you fire up your browser, it may take you to a *landing page* instead of to the site you want to go to. Landing pages tell you what you have to do to get onto a network—like enter your credit card info and cough up a few bucks.

- **Secure networks.** You need a password to get onto these networks. If you're at a coffee shop, ask the kid behind the counter; at work, ask one of the IT guys. As with open networks, not all of these connections are free: You may have to sign up for a subscription or fork over a payment.

The next two sections teach you how to connect to both kinds of WiFi networks.

Connect to an open network

This process is pretty simple:

❶ Open the Wi-Fi application by tapping the Wi-Fi icon  **in the Launcher.** Alternatively, open WiFi through the network menu in the status bar. If you go that route, tap Wi-Fi→Wi-Fi Preferences. Either way, the Pre displays a list of all the WiFi networks it finds. Closed networks with some type of security feature have a little padlock next to their names. Skip to the next section to learn how to connect to one of those networks.

❷ In the network list, tap the name of the one you want to connect to. If you don't see the network you have in mind, tap Join Network and type in its name. If the Pre can't find it, you'll see a message that says "No network of that name with that security setting was found."

❸ Make sure the Security box for the network you just chose says Open. If not, tap on whatever it says in the Security box (which is either "WPA-personal", "WEP", or "Enterprise"). When you do so, you see these three security options listed, along with "Open". Tap "Open".

❹ Tap Connect. Unless you hit a snag and can't connect for some reason, you're good to go. If you do hit a snag, the problem might be with the network itself, so contact the person who set it up.

Connect to a secure network

Getting onto a secure network can take a few more steps, and you need to have login info for the network:

❶ **Open the Wi-Fi application.** See step 1 in the previous list.

❷ **If the network you want is on the list, tap its name and enter your user name and password.** Then tap Sign In and you're done.

❸ **If the network isn't listed, tap Join Other Network.** Enter the network's name.

❹ **Tap the Security box.** Depending on the type of security the network uses—you may have to ask the person who set up the network what kind it is—tap WPA-personal, WEP, or Enterprise.

❺ **Tap Connect.** Fill in your user name, password, certificate (a digital document used for authentication), and any other info it requests.

> **Tip** You can customize a WiFi network so that the *IP address* (the address assigned to your network) is automatically configured: Tap the network's name, and then tap the "Automatic IP settings" switch so that it's on. If automatic IP settings are turned off, you have to manually fill in the IP Address and the *Subnet Address* (part of a network typically confined to a geographic location, like a single plant in a big company).

⑥ **Tap Sign In.** If everything checks out, the Pre connects to the network, and a checkmark appears in the list next to its name.

Even after you disconnect from a network because you're no longer in range, that network stays on your list of known hotspots. The Pre is smart about reconnecting you to networks you've used before: When you turn on Wi-Fi, the phone scans for the last network you used and automatically connects to it. If you're connected to one network but would rather use another, just open the Wi-Fi Preferences menu and tap the other network's name.

To remove a network from the list of ones the Pre knows about, open Wi-Fi, tap the network's name, and tap Forget Network. You might do this if you change jobs. Just remember that if you want to connect to that network again, you'll have to re-enter all the relevant sign-on information.

Use the Pre Browser

Imagine taking the web browser you use on your PC or Mac and putting it through some Tom Thumb contraption to shrink it down so it fits on a 3.1-inch screen. That's basically what the Pre browser is—a smaller version of your regular browser. You still get swanky graphics, eye-popping pictures, and some video, just on a smaller screen.

> **Note** The Pre's browser can handle most of the same content as regular browsers, but it doesn't understand Flash or Java technology. (Support was said to be coming for a standard known as Flash 10, so video that doesn't work at the time this book was published might work by the time you read this.) That just means some of the videos you can watch on your computer won't play on the Pre.

To open the Pre browser (a.k.a. the Web application), tap the ⬤ icon in the Launcher. The first time you do this, you see thumbnail-sized icons, which, as you'll learn later in this chapter, are bookmarks for popular websites like Facebook, MySpace, Amazon, and ESPN, along with icons for the Palm and Sprint sites. Tap one of the icons to jump to that site.

To go elsewhere, type a web address (known to geeks as a *URL*—Uniform Resource Locator) in the bar at the top of the screen. You can scroll up to the address bar, but if you don't see it, just start typing, and the bar drops down like a curtain.

Fortunately, you don't need to enter the *http://www* part of any web address. To go to the Onion humor site, for example, just type *onion.com*. Then press the Enter key ⬅ or tap the arrow to the right of the address bar, and you go to that website.

As you start typing, the Pre suggests sites you've visited before that start with the same letters. If the site you want shows up on the list, tap its name to go there. If you type the wrong thing, just press backspace ⬅ on the keyboard and try again.

Search the Web

The Pre is good at helping you find what you want online. If you're in the Launcher or Card view and want to go to a web page, start typing its name, and universal search (page 46) kicks in. When you've entered the term you want to search for, tap the word "Google" to go to the popular search engine, "Wikipedia" to jump to that massive online encyclopedia, "Google Maps" (page 171) to get directions for where you're going, or "Twitter".

Tip Twitter is a wildly popular "micro-blogging" site where you can share your thoughts—as long as they're 140 characters or fewer. You can download such Twitter applications as Tweed from Pivotal Labs and Spaz from Funkatron Productions from the App Catalog (see page 225).

Get Around Online

You rarely sit still on the web: You read part of a page and want to look over something else. Or you want to go back to the last page you looked at, or skip to another site you perused earlier. Here are some ways to jump around:

- Tap the left arrow ◀ in the browser to move back to the last page you viewed. Keep tapping it to move back through more pages, or use the back gesture described on page 27.

- After you've gone back to a previously viewed page, tap the right arrow ➡ to move forward again.

- Tap ↻ to refresh the current page—to get updated stock quotes or sports scores, say.

Fancy Finger Work

It's time to apply the techniques you learned in Chapter 2 (page 26) to the web. Here's how:

- **Scrolling.** Swipe up or down on the screen to go to the top or bottom of a page. If you scroll to the top of the page, you'll see a banner with the page's title.

Tip Tapping the banner at the top of the page (which you may have to scroll up to see) displays the page's web address, which you can copy and paste into a memo or text message.

- **Zooming.** Zoom in on a page by pinching out—pressing two fingers against the screen and spreading them apart. To zoom out, bring your fingers back together in a pinching-in motion.

- **Double-tap.** If you want to read a specific area of a web page, double-tap it. The area you tapped moves to the center and takes up the whole screen.

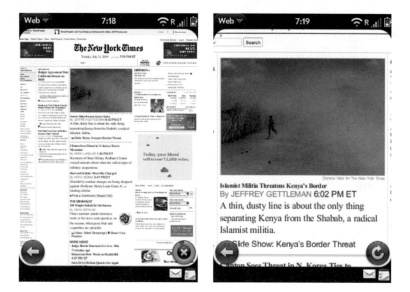

- **Rotate the Pre.** Turn the Pre on its side to change the screen's orientation from portrait mode (long and skinny) to landscape mode (short and fat). This is handy when you try to look at a picture that's too wide to fit on the screen when the Pre is vertical. With the display horizontal, you can swipe up and down the gesture area (page 18) to scroll up and down a page. Fun fact: You can even turn the Pre upside-down, and the page will appear right-side-up.

- **Do the Pan.** Tap, hold and drag a page to pan around it.

Tip If you need to fill out a web form—to log into your online bank account, for example—tap the boxes on the screen to position your cursor and type in the required info. Then press Enter ⬅ to complete the drill.

Links

As you know, links take you from one online spot to another, like from one article to a related story. Links usually appear in blue text, but they can be a little hard to tap on the Pre. Zooming in or double-tapping on a page (as explained above) makes it a lot simpler to tap on links. If a phone number in a web page is a link, tapping it brings up the Pre's dial pad with the number already entered, so you can call it by simply tapping the green phone button (see page 76).

Open More Browser Windows

Say you're doing some research on one site and want to check out another site's opinion. No problem: You can open a second (or third, or fourth, and so on) browser window. From the browser's application menu, tap New Card. The page you were just on steps aside and gets replaced by a new window. Simply enter the address for the second site.

The page that moved out of the way is still open. To move between sites, tap the center button to switch to Card view, and then scroll to and tap the page you want to revisit.

You can also open a link on a web page in a new window by holding down the orange and space keys on the keyboard and tapping the link.

Share a Web Page

Say you find a cool website you want to tell your friends about. No problem: With the Pre browser open to the page, go to the application menu and tap Page→Share. The Email application opens to a mostly completed new email. The subject line (which you can change) reads "Check out this web page…" The body of the message reads, "Hey you gotta check out…" followed by a link to the site you're sharing; a picture of the site is attached to the email for good measure. Type the recipient's address in the To area, tweak the message or subject line if you want, and then send the message just as you would any other email (see page 133).

Add a Web Page to the Launcher

If you go to a certain site over and over— one with a train schedule, say—you can add it to the Launcher. With the Pre browser open to the page you want to add, go to the application menu and tap Page→"Add to Launcher". A new page appears showing an icon for the page, its title, and its web address. To customize any of these, just tap them.

Why might you want to edit the page's address? Maybe you chose a page within the site (*www.cnn.com/politics*, for example), but then decide you'd rather add the site's home page (*www.cnn.com*) to the Launcher.

When everything looks good, tap the "Add to Launcher" button at the bottom of the screen. Or, if you change your mind about the whole thing, tap Cancel.

> **Tip** To remove a page from the Launcher once you add it, hold down the orange button on the keyboard and tap the Launcher icon. Tap the Delete button that appears, or Done if you decide to keep it. You'll be asked to tap Delete a second time to confirm your intention to remove the page from the Launcher.

Create Bookmarks

When you launch the Web application, the first page you see always shows icons for various sites. Each icon is a *bookmark,* which is basically a link to a website—just tap one of the icons to jump to the corresponding site. As mentioned on page 160, Palm has already chosen several bookmarks for you, but you can edit those and add your own.

You can have as many bookmarks as you like on the Pre, but only a dozen appear on this opening browser page (and you may have to scroll down to see the one you want). To create a bookmark, open the page you want to have handy, and then go to the application menu and tap Add Bookmark. A screen similar to the one that appears when you add a web page to the Launcher shows up, with an icon—it's a tiny picture of part of the page, title, and web address. Tap the Add Bookmark button to complete the task, or Cancel if you decide that the page isn't worth it after all.

You can control what this bookmark looks like. If you don't like the image the Pre uses automatically, tap the bookmark icon. You'll see the web page you bookmarked behind a small white square. Tap, hold, and drag the web page until the part of the page you want to use as the icon fills the white square. Spread and pinch your fingers to get it just right. When it looks good, tap Done.

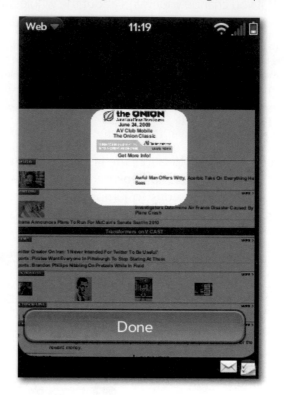

You can also edit the web address and title the Pre has given the bookmark. Simply tap those fields. When you're satisfied, tap Add Bookmark to finish up and make the Pre add the new bookmark to the Web application's start page (if there's room for it there).

After you create a bookmark, you've got two ways to jump to a bookmarked page:

- Tap any of the dozen bookmark icons on the Web program's start page.

- From within the Web application, go to the application menu and tap Bookmarks and then tap the bookmark you want to open. That's how you access bookmarks that didn't make the cut among the top 12—and also where you need to go to edit any of your bookmarks, as explained in the next section.

Edit bookmarks

Here's how to change or delete bookmarks:

- **Edit.** Tap the circled *i* to the right of the bookmark's name, and then tweak the icon, address, or title as just described.

- **Change the order.** Drag the bookmark up or down the list. The top 12 bookmarks on the list are the ones that appear on the Web application's start page.

- **Delete.** To get rid of a bookmark, throw it off the side of the screen, and then tap Delete.

Consult Your Browsing History

Say you want to go back to a website you looked at the other day, but you didn't bookmark it, and you can't remember its address. Fortunately, you can consult your web history to jog your memory.

In the Web program's application menu, tap History to see a list of all the sites you visited during the past three weeks. Scroll through the list to find the page you want, and then tap its name to hop straight to it. Easy, huh?

If you don't want anyone else to know where you've been, clear your history (and free up a little memory to boot). From the application menu, tap Preferences→Clear History.

Advanced Browser Settings

You can do a few more things to customize the browser. To find the following settings, open the application menu and tap Preferences:

- **Block Popups.** As you probably know, *pop-ups* are web pages that, well, pop up unexpectedly, like snakes in the grass. They're typically really obnoxious advertisements. As a general rule, keep the Block Popups switch set to Yes. But if you visit a site and can't see the info you want, like your stock portfolio, web forms, or a picture—anything that might open in a separate window—turn Block Popups off by tapping this switch. You probably want to change it back to Yes when you're done.

- **Accept Cookies.** *Cookies* are tiny bits of data that the sites you visit put on your Pre so they can recognize you when you come back. Cookies are usually harmless, but with all the talk of privacy nowadays, no one would blame you for worrying about them. So you can turn cookies on or off any time by tapping the Accept Cookies switch (it's automatically set to Yes unless you change it). Just be aware that if you have cookies turned off, some web pages may not load properly.

- **JavaScript.** Programmers use *JavaScript* (a programming language) to add a touch of pizzazz to some web pages, like making images react when you mouse over them. As with cookies, turning off this setting may also prevent some web pages from loading correctly. Out of the box, this setting is turned on; tap it to turn JavaScript off.

- **Clear History.** As explained in the previous section, tap this button to clear your browsing history.

- **Clear Cookies.** By tapping this button, you can remove all the cookies from your Pre.

- **Clear Cache.** Some web pages leave remnants of your last visit on your Pre so the page loads much faster when you drop by again. The place where they store this info is called a *cache.* If you're tight on storage space or worried about security, tap Clear Cache to scrub away those remains, free up space, and wash away your security concerns. It's not a bad idea to do this fairly often. (To check how much available space you have left on your Pre, tap the Device Info icon in the Launcher.)

Pinpoint Your Location

GPS (Global Positioning System) capability, which uses signals from orbiting satellites to pinpoint your location, was once reserved for pricey car navigation systems. But in recent years that spiffy technology has gone mainstream: You can find it all over the place, including on your Pre.

> **Note** While GPS gives you the most accurate results, the Pre also uses signals from cellphone towers and WiFi hotspots to figure out where you are. These three technologies work together to balance precision, speed, and power consumption in figuring out your whereabouts.

Yep, the Pre can double as one of those great-to-have-when-you're-lost navigation systems—you'll learn how on page 175. But it also uses GPS technology in several other ways: in web applications like Google Maps, by *geotagging* (adding location info to) the pictures you shoot (page 215), and in various other programs you can get from the App Catalog.

When you first set up your Pre (see page 223), it asked if you wanted to use *Location Services,* the term for the technology that GPS programs use. If you said yes, the Pre is already gathering your location behind the scenes. If you said no, you can turn it on any time by tapping on the Location Services icon in the Launcher. When you do, you'll see these settings:

- **Auto Locate.** If this setting is turned off, you see a message each time you open an application that wants to use your location to figure out where you are and what might be around you. The message asks "Allow the Google Maps application to use Location Services for this session?" (If you use a program other than Google Maps, the message will have the name of that program in place of "Google Maps.") If it's on, such programs automatically determine and use your location.

- **Use GPS.** This setting has to be on for the Pre to more precisely determine your location than it can by using signals from cellphone towers and WiFi hotspots. But GPS doesn't work when you're indoors, and it drains your battery, so turn this setting off when you're not planning to use a location program.

- **Geotag Photos.** You won't see this option if you've turned off Auto Locate. When you use the Pre's camera with this setting turned on, the Pre adds location coordinates to pictures you shoot. This is called *geotagging*—see page 215 to learn more about it.

- **Background Data Collection.** With this setting on, Google anonymously collects location data (through Google Maps on the Pre) that it says improves the quality of Location Services. If you think that's creepy or a violation of your privacy, keep this setting turned off.

Google Maps and Traffic

Google Maps and GPS make a potent combination, especially when you add the Pre's awesome universal search feature to the mix. You may never have to ask a stranger for directions again.

Hungry? Or did your car break down on a rural road? No sweat: The Pre can tell where you are and find restaurants, mechanics, or basically any address that's close by. Google Maps will not only tell you how to get there, but also let you know if you'll hit any traffic on the way.

Browse Google Maps

The Google Maps application comes preinstalled on your Pre. To launch it, tap its icon in the Launcher. If the Pre doesn't know your location when you open Google Maps, it displays a map of the U.S. (you can drag it to see other parts of the world—but it's not going to do you much good if the Pre doesn't know where you are). If it *can* pinpoint your whereabouts, you see a local map instead. As with any web page, you can pan around maps by dragging your finger, double-tap to zoom in and out, and spread or pinch your fingers to magnify what's on the screen or to make it shrink.

A pulsating blue dot on the screen identifies where Google thinks you are. If the dot is inside a light-blue circle, that means Google isn't totally sure about your whereabouts, but it's making its best guess. If you don't see the blue dot because you dragged the map around and veered off course, tap ● at the bottom of the screen to make the map hop to your location, centered on the screen.

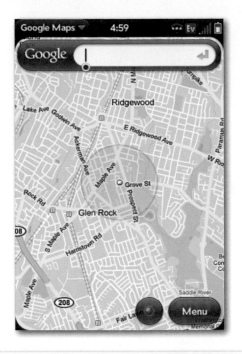

Note If you've turned off Location Services (page 170), the dot at the bottom of the screen is grayed out.

Tap the Menu button at the bottom of the Google Maps screen to see these options:

- **Search Map.** When you choose this option, a box appears near the top of the Maps screen where you can type in a Zip code or address, enter a search term like *Coffee Canton, Ohio*, or run a universal search—go to page 46 to learn how.

- **Show Traffic.** When you select this item, your Pre displays a map of your local area that includes current traffic conditions. Green roads mean traffic's flowing at over 50 mph; yellow means 25–50 mph; and red means you want to take a different route, as traffic's moving at less than 25 mph—if at all. If a road appears in gray, Google doesn't know what traffic there is like. When you have the traffic feature turned on, this menu option changes to Hide Traffic.

Note Google says it offers real-time traffic for more than 30 U.S. cities, with partial coverage in other cities around the world.

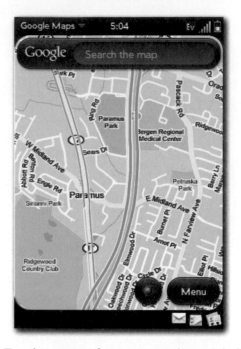

- **Satellite View.** Tap this option for a spectacular aerial photo of your location. Double-tap the screen or spread your fingers to zoom closer to your own roof.

- **Get Directions.** Choose this item to find out how to go from where you are (or from anywhere, actually) to another spot. The next section has more about getting from here to there.

- **Help & Terms.** If you're worried about how Google uses your information, you can read these sleep-inducing lawyerly disclaimers.

- **Clear Map.** Select this option to get rid of directions and businesses you've searched for, so you can start anew; the next section tells you how to search.

- **Close Menu.** This takes you back to your map.

Use Google Maps with Search

You can find a location on the map by entering it in the search box at the top of the map screen. Or you can start a search without even opening the Google Maps application: As you learned on page 46, universal search kicks in the moment you start typing.

Suppose you're craving a tuna roll. Start typing *sushi* on the keyboard. Once your Pre gets past all the "Susans" in your Contacts lists and recognizes you're on another mission, it brings up the main universal search screen with buttons for Google, Google Maps, Wikipedia, and Twitter. Tap Google Maps, and the application slides up from the bottom of the screen and displays a map of your current location, with red droplets indicating all the sushi restaurants it finds in your area.

The droplet closest to you has a black dot in it, and the name of the restaurant it represents is listed at the top of the screen. If you want to try a different restaurant, tap another droplet to move the black dot and see that joint's info instead. Alternatively, you can tap the left and right arrows that appear on either side of the restaurant's name at the top of the screen.

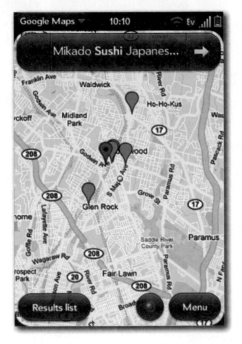

To learn more about a restaurant you selected, tap its name. Up pops a screen with the address and phone number of the place. From there, you can:

- **Tap the phone number** to make the dial pad pop up so you can call and make a reservation.

- **Tap "See on map" or the bottom-left Map button** to return to the map view.

- **Tap "Directions to here"**, and a new screen appears with the address of the restaurant in the To field. You can get directions to it from your current location or from another spot by entering a new address or Zip code in the From section.

With the addresses in place, tap the Directions button. You can toggle between a step-by-step list of directions and a map view by tapping the Map button that took the place of the Directions button. In map view, tap the arrows in the banner at the top of the screen to get the next instruction. A green droplet shows where you are right now, and a red droplet represents your destination.

Sprint Navigation

Google Maps is a terrific application, but it's missing one major feature that car navigation systems have: It can't talk. The Sprint Navigation application fills that void. Unlike such programs on other phones, you don't have to pay a subscription fee to use Sprint Navigation—it's included as part of your Sprint data plan. Once you get it set up, the application can use a robotic female voice to tell you where to go: "Turn left in .4 miles on Prospect St."

> **Tip** You may want to keep the car radio turned down to hear the directions. Even with the Pre's volume cranked all the way up, they're sometimes difficult to hear. But they chime in fairly often, giving you plenty of warning before you have to make the next turn.

To open the Sprint Navigation application, tap its icon in the Launcher. When it opens, you'll be prompted to turn on Location Services (page 170) if they're not already on.

As with Google Maps, you can pan and zoom around Sprint Navigation maps and get traffic info. You can even display a map in 3-D if you want, something Google Maps can't do; page 178 tells you how. To get directions, tap Drive To in the menu that appears when you open the application, and then enter a destination (a specific address or business name, for example), or pick an address from the Pre's Contacts list (page 61).

Add any destinations you frequent to a favorites list. For example, you can add your home and office address, since they're often your starting points. To add a favorite, in the main menu, tap Share & More→My Favorites. You'll see a list of any favorites you already added. Tap the add favorite button ✚ at the bottom of the screen to bring up an Add Favorite screen with choices for finding an address from Recent Places (where you've been lately), Address (type one in), Business (search by category near your current location), Airport, or Contact (tapping here brings up a list of your contacts).

You can also use the program to search for all kinds of places, like restaurants, gas stations (and gas by price), ATMs, WiFi hotspots (page 155), parking lots, hospitals, and shopping malls. To do that, choose Search from the main menu, and then tap the Category box to identify what you're looking for; decide whether to search near your current location or another spot. You can also type in a search term at the top of the screen, though searching that way doesn't always give you very good results.

As you drive around, the screen displays how far you are from your destination and when you'll likely arrive there, just like grownup (and more expensive) car navigation systems.

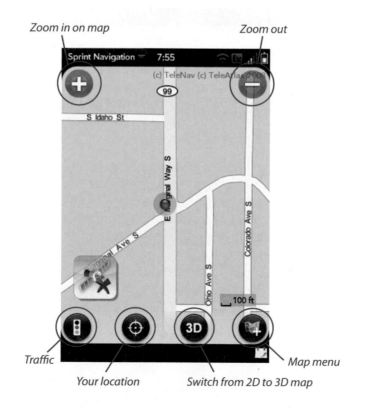

Zoom in on map   Zoom out

Traffic   Map menu

Your location   Switch from 2D to 3D map

As with most applications, you can tweak some settings to make Sprint Navigation behave the way you want. Go to the application menu and tap Preferences, or go to the main Sprint Navigation menu you saw when you first opened the application and tap Share & More→Preferences.

Here are the different options you have:

- **Route Style.** You can choose the fastest or shortest route to where you're going, or get directions that Sprint says will minimize traffic delays. Alternatively, you can indicate whether you prefer highways to streets or vice versa. And if you plan on walking, you can choose a pedestrian route. If you want the app to ask you which route style you want before each trip, tap "Ask me each trip" instead. You can choose only one route style.

- **Distance Units.** If you're driving in the U.S., tap Miles/Feet. If you're driving in most other parts of the globe, tap Kilometers/Meters.

- **Moving Maps.** Here you can choose between fancy 3-D maps (the default) or plain-vanilla 2-D maps. 3-D looks nicer, but 2-D may be easier to follow.

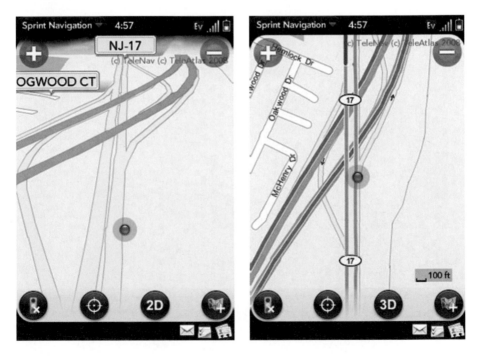

- **Audio.** You don't have to make the program talk, but if you choose to have the female voice guide you, here's where you choose whether to have her say street names or leave them out. Tap the selection your want: With Street Names, No Street Names, or No Audio.

- **Backlight.** If you turn on this setting, the Pre leaves the screen on instead of dimming it after 30 seconds, so you can see the maps as you go. (Of course, you should keep your eyes on the road when you're driving.) The downside to turning this on is that it eats up a lot of battery power.

- **Traffic Alerts.** With this setting turned on, the program gives you visual traffic alerts, as well as audio ones if you have the voice feature turned on. Alerts show up on both 2-D and 3-D maps. Alternate routes are sometimes suggested through a button that may appear on the corner of the screen.

- **Call-In Number.** This is the number to call Sprint to get an address, as explained in the Tip on page 176.

Chapter

8

The Pre as Media Center

The Pre excels at making and receiving phone calls. You can also use it to browse the Web with the best of 'em. And you rely on it for your email, messaging, and event reminders. If you didn't know better, you might think your Pre was all work and no play.

But you *can* use the Pre for all kinds of fun stuff. In this chapter, you'll learn how to add songs and video to it, how to buy music online, and how to watch YouTube videos and even TV on your Pre.

Add Media to the Pre

The steps for adding media to the Pre are basically the same whether you fill it up with music, videos, or photos. (You'll learn about adding photos in the chapter on the Pre's camera, coming up next.) There are a couple of ways to do so. One is to automatically sync the media files on your computer with your Pre, and the other is to manually transfer files from your computer to the Pre. To add music, you have a third option: You can buy songs online. This section covers all your options.

Note When the Pre first came out, you could use Apple's iTunes software to sync media files between the Pre and your PC (via the Pre's Media Sync feature). In July 2009, Apple changed iTunes, to block this capability. Just before this book went to press, Palm, through a software update, restored the Pre's ability to work with iTunes. It's quite likely that this cat-and-mouse game between Apple and Palm will continue. By the time you read this, you may or may not be able to use Media Sync and iTunes to sync your media files. If you can, follow the instructions in "Sync Music and Video Files" section below. If not, you can still transfer songs, videos, and photos to your Pre; follow the directions under "Copy Media Files from Your Computer" further along in this chapter.

Sync Music and Video Files

You can sync media files on your computer—whether it's Windows-based or a Mac—the same way you sync them when you have an iPod: using Apple's popular iTunes software. In fact, when you connect your Pre to a computer, iTunes treats the Pre as though it were an iPod. (Don't worry: If you don't have iTunes installed on your computer, you can still get media files onto your Pre; skip to page 184 to learn how.)

Note Even though you may be able to use iTunes to sync your music library, iTunes isn't the Pre's music player (in fact, iTunes isn't even installed on your Pre—it's on your desktop or laptop PC). The Pre comes with its own MP3 player, listed in the Launcher as Music.

To sync your media files, connect the Pre to your computer using the Pre's USB cable. When you link the two, the Pre displays three buttons: Media Sync, USB Drive, and Just Charge. Tap Media Sync (you'll learn about the USB Drive option in a moment; Just Charge—well, that recharges your Pre).

Two things happen the first time you tap Media Sync: First, iTunes automatically opens on your computer and turns on the "Open iTunes when this iPod is attached" checkbox. From this point on, whenever you connect your Pre to your computer and hit Media Sync, iTunes opens and automatically syncs your music and video libraries. (If you want to control the action, in iTunes, click the "Open iTunes..." checkbox to turn it off and then follow these steps: connect your Pre, tap Media Sync, and then open iTunes manually on your computer.)

The second thing that happens is that iTunes' new-device screen appears, giving you the chance to rename your phone; iTunes automatically lists it as "Palm Pre."

 Note When you disconnect the Pre from your desktop, don't simply yank out the USB cable because this could corrupt some—or even all—of your files. (It's unlikely, but it could happen.) On a Windows machine, disconnect the Pre by right-clicking the drive that represents your phone and then clicking Eject. On a Mac, drag the drive representing the Pre to the Trash. Then you can safely unplug the cable.

Once connected, your Pre appears as an icon (along with its name) in iTunes' Devices list. Click it and iTunes' sync screen opens. This is your control panel for syncing media files.

Note You can sync music and video files whether they originate on a Windows or Mac PC. The Pre handles any reformatting necessary to make sure the files play properly on your smartphone.

You can either sync all your songs, playlists, and video files or pick just certain files to sync. To import music files, on the iTunes sync screen, click the Music tab. Check the box for "All Songs and Playlists" to import all your music (except ones that have restrictions on them, as explained in the Note below), or check the Selected Playlists to narrow down your sync.

Note You can only import media files that don't have Digital Rights Management (DRM) copy restrictions. Though Apple has recently shifted its focus to DRM-free material, many older songs you bought through iTunes' music store are DRM-protected and can't make their way to your Pre. Most commercial movies of any note—and even many obscure ones—are also copy protected. As of this writing, that doesn't leave you with much. But you can still sync any homegrown movies that may be in your iTunes library.

If you have a large music collection that won't fit on your Pre, you need to parc down the songs you import. In fact, iTunes displays a message telling you that you don't have enough room on your Pre to fit 'em all, and graciously offers to delete some photos and albums to free up space. You can click Yes or No.

If you click No (the better option), on the iTunes' Summary screen, check "Sync only checked songs and video" and then cherry-pick the songs and music videos you want to export by going into the iTunes library and checking off the songs you want to bring over to the Pre.

The process for syncing video files is similar: On the iTunes sync screen, tap the Movies tab. You'll have the option to sync all your movies or just selected ones. You can narrow down your selection to all of the unwatched movies on your list, the most recently watched movies, or the 3, 5 or 10 most-watched movies. But it's worth pointing out again that just about all commercial movies in your iTunes library will never make it to the Pre because of DRM protection (see the Note above).

Copy Media Files from Your Computer

To transfer music and video files, connect the Pre to your desktop or laptop PC using the Pre's USB cable. When you link the two, the Pre displays three buttons: Media Sync, USB Drive, and Just Charge. Tap USB Drive. The computer treats the Pre as though it were an external hard drive. (On the Pre, you'll see an illustration of a portable hard drive, with a USB symbol on it.)

Then select the files you want to transfer. How you do that depends on what kind of computer you have:

• **On a Windows XP machine,** open My Computer and look in the My Music folder for songs. Windows XP typically stores videos in a My Videos folder, though you should also check the My Pictures folder, where you might find other videos you shot.

• **On a Windows Vista computer,** open Computer and look in the Music folder for songs. Vista usually stores videos in a Videos folder, though, again, you might find some in Vista's Pictures folder.

• **On a Mac,** open the Finder and look in the Music and Movies folders.

Name	Artists	Album	#	Genre	Rating
01 - Mack the Knife.mp3	Ella Fitzgerald	Compact Jazz: Ella Fit...	1	Vocal	
02 - Desafinado (Off K...	Ella Fitzgerald	Compact Jazz: Ella Fit...	2	Vocal	
03 - You'll Have to Swi...	Ella Fitzgerald	Compact Jazz: Ella Fit...	3	Vocal	
04 - I Can't Get Started...	Ella Fitzgerald	Compact Jazz: Ella Fit...	4	Vocal	
05 - A Night in Tunisia....	Ella Fitzgerald	Compact Jazz: Ella Fit...	5	Vocal	
06 - A-Tisket, A-Tasket...	Ella Fitzgerald	Compact Jazz: Ella Fit...	6	Vocal	
07 - Shiny Stockings.m...	Ella Fitzgerald	Compact Jazz: Ella Fit...	7	Vocal	
08 - Smooth Sailing.mp3	Ella Fitzgerald	Compact Jazz: Ella Fit...	8	Vocal	
09 - Goody Goody.mp3	Ella Fitzgerald	Compact Jazz: Ella Fit...	9	Vocal	
10 - Rough Ridin'.mp3	Ella Fitzgerald	Compact Jazz: Ella Fit...	10	Vocal	
11 - The Girl from Ipan...	Ella Fitzgerald	Compact Jazz: Ella Fit...	11	Vocal	
12 - Sweet Georgia Bro...	Ella Fitzgerald	Compact Jazz: Ella Fit...	12	Vocal	
13 - Duke's Place.mp3	Ella Fitzgerald	Compact Jazz: Ella Fit...	13	Vocal	
14 - Misty.mp3	Ella Fitzgerald	Compact Jazz: Ella Fit...	14	Vocal	
15 - Somebody Loves ...	Ella Fitzgerald	Compact Jazz: Ella Fit...	15	Vocal	
16 - How High the Mo...	Ella Fitzgerald	Compact Jazz: Ella Fit...	16	Vocal	

 Tip To help locate videos on your computer, search for files with the .mp4, .m4v, .m4a, .mov, .3gp, and .3g2 file extensions.

Once you select your files, drag them to the Pre, which appears as a drive under My Computer in XP, Computer in Vista, and Devices in a Mac's Finder.

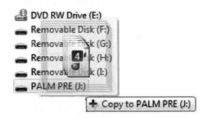

Drag the media files you selected to the Pre, listed as an external drive

Sync from Windows Media Player

If you have a Windows-based computer, you have another way to transfer files: by using Windows Media Player's Sync feature.

First, connect the Pre to your computer with the USB cable as explained on page 184. Then open Windows Media Player by double-clicking the program's desktop icon (if you have one) or finding it under All Programs. In Windows Media Player, click the Sync menu at the top of the screen, and then click Palm Pre in the drop-down list. Then click Set Up Sync.

The first time you connect the Pre to Windows Media Player, the player figures out which sync method will work best—it depends on the size of your library and storage capacity:

- If you have at least 4 GB free and your entire library can fit on the Pre, Windows Media Player automatically syncs your whole library. After that, when you connect the two devices, Windows Media Player updates the Pre to match the contents of your computer's library.

- If you get close to the Pre's storage capacity when you sync files from a Windows PC, Windows gives you the option of deleting all the media files from your Pre before it continues copying the files. Unless you don't care about the files that will get erased, a better option (and the default) is to leave the existing files on the Pre and just use the available space. (You can always delete files later.) Click Next to proceed with the sync. Windows translates as many files to the Pre as space allows and then stops.

Buy Music Through Amazon

Palm doesn't run a media store like Apple does with iTunes. But there's a good—and often cheaper—alternative: Amazon MP3, Amazon.com's music-download program. Your Pre comes with Amazon MP3 already installed (you can find it in the Launcher).

Here are a couple things to keep in mind about using Amazon MP3:

- **You need an Amazon.com account to buy music.** If you have an account for buying books, you're all set—use the same email address and password. If not, go to *www.amazon.com* and sign up for a free account.

    When you open the Amazon MP3 program—tap 🔳 in the Launcher—you don't have to sign in to browse, but you do if you want to buy anything. To sign in right away, go to the application menu and tap Sign In, enter your email address and Amazon.com password, and then tap the Sign In button at the bottom of the screen.

    Amazon MP3 supports the same 1-Click buying feature Amazon.com does, so once you're signed in, if you tap the Buy button for a track, 1-Click lets you skip having to enter your password.

- **You have to be connected to WiFi (page 42) to download music.** While connected to Sprint's 3G network (page 154), you can preview music and queue up songs you want to buy, but to actually *download* a song, you need to be connected to a WiFi hotspot (page 155) because of a restriction placed on Amazon by the people who own the rights to the music.

Browse the Amazon catalog

You can riffle through Amazon's music collection from the Amazon MP3 program's main screen in several ways:

- **Search Amazon MP3.** When you open the program, the first thing you see is a search box. Type in a song, album, or artist name, and then press Enter ⏎.

- **By genre.** Amazon MP3 initially displays all genres of music, but you can tap the menu bar at the top of the screen to pick a specific genre (Alternative Rock, Blues, and so on). Scroll down the list to see all your choices.

- **New & Notable.** The program displays thumbnails of 10 new album covers on the main screen. Swipe left or right to browse through the list. If you change music genres as described above, the New & Notables recommendations change, too.

- **Top 100.** Amazon tracks the top 100 releases in several categories (New Releases, Albums, Artists, and Songs) and provides links to each list on the main Amazon MP3 screen. When you tap a name in the Top 100 Artists list, you see a list of all the musician's albums and songs for sale on Amazon. A drop-down menu in the bar at the top of the screen lets you sort their work by album or song, and you'll find bios for prominent artists.

Preview and buy songs

As you browse through Amazon MP3, tap a song name to play a 30-second preview.

Songs typically cost 89¢ to 99¢ each. When you're ready to buy one, tap its price button, which turns green and changes to read "Buy". Tap again to buy the song and check out. (If you haven't signed into your Amazon account yet, you'll go to a Sign In page before the checkout page.)

> **Note** Amazon doesn't waste any time: If you're signed into your account when you tap Buy, Amazon charges your credit card right away.

If you're connected to WiFi, the song starts downloading. Tap Download to see the download's progress—it takes several seconds to get a whole song. If you change your mind and need to cancel a download, tap the X next to the song that's downloading.

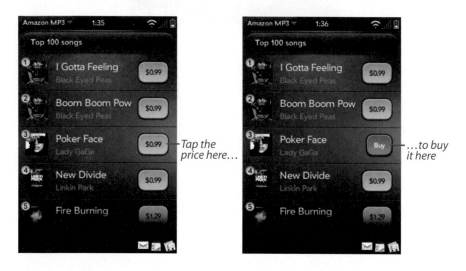

Tap the price here… …to buy it here

You have to open the Music application to listen to your new purchase, as explained in the next section.

> **Tip** If the Pre's Media Sync feature is available (see the Note on page 181) and you want to transfer music you bought through Amazon MP3 to iTunes on your desktop or laptop PC, download the Palm Music Assistant program, which automates the process. Choose the PC or Mac version at *http://palm.com/music-assistant*. If Media Sync is unavailable, the Palm Music Assistant won't do you any good, but you can still manually drag the files into iTunes using the USB Drive option (see page 184).

The Pre's MP3 Player

Not long ago, music fans had to carry around an MP3 player *and* a cellphone. Eventually, cellphones could play music, too, but they couldn't *rock!* Well, the Pre rocks.

It comes with 8 gigabytes of storage. Once you take into account the Pre's built-in programs and an average library of third-party programs, as well as your photos, and videos, you should still have enough room for more than 1,000 songs.

> **Note** The Pre can play music directly from the Internet (called *streaming*) or play songs you've copied onto it as long as they're in one of the following file formats: AAC (iTunes' format), AAC+, and MP3. If you get a music file as an email attachment, the Pre can open it if it's in AAC, AAC+, AMR, MP3, QCLEP, or WAV format.

To listen to all these songs, the Pre includes its own MP3 player, which you find in the Launcher. Open it by tapping the Music icon .

> **Tip** You're not exactly rocking when you listen to music through the Pre's tinny, mono speaker. For the full stereo effect, don the earbuds that came with your Pre, or better yet, plug in your favorite set of stereo headphones.

The playback controls on the Pre will be familiar to anyone who's ever had an MP3 player (or a Sony Walkman, for that matter). Tap a song to play it, and a set of buttons appears at the bottom of the screen. Here's what they do:

- **Play ▶/Pause ❚❚.** When a song is playing, you can tap the ❚❚ button to stop playback. When you do, it turns into a play button, ▶; tap it to start the music where you paused it. As noted on page 9, you can also press the button on the Pre's headphones to toggle between play and pause.

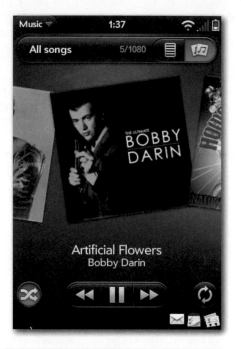

> **Tip** Crank up or lower the volume by pressing the volume buttons on the left side of the Pre. Bars that temporarily appear on the screen show how high you've turned it up.

- **Previous/Rewind ◀◀.** This is one fickle control. When you tap this button, the player sometimes retreats to the previous track and sometimes jumps to the start of the *current* track (at which point, if you wanted the previous track, you have to tap Previous/Rewind again). But it's hard to know which response you'll get when you tap this button. If you're near the start of a song, it'll go back one track; if you're farther along in a track, it'll jump to the beginning of the song you're listening to.

  If you press and hold this button, the player rapidly plays the song backward; release it to play the song from that point.

- **Fast Forward** ▶▶. Tap this button to skip to the next track, or hold it down to fast-forward within a track.

Tip There's an even easier way to skip or repeat tracks on the Pre. In Album Art view (page 193), flick the song's album cover to the left or right to play the next or previous song.

- **Shuffle the playlist** ⤬. Tapping this button makes the Pre play the current playlist in random order. When you turn on Shuffle, the button turns blue.

- **Repeat** ↻. Tap ↻ to repeat the *playlist* (page 192) you're listening to (the button turns blue). Tap a second time to repeat just the *song* you're listening to (the button turns blue and a "1" appears in the middle). Tap the button again to turn off repeat.

Note The Pre plays music even after the touch screen is locked and even when the ringer switch is off.

If you play music while you're in a program or in Card view, music notes appear in the notifications area. If you tap the notes, the Pre displays the current song's name and a set of miniature playback controls in the notifications area.

As long as you have the Music application open, you'll see the music-note icon, even if you pause playback. Tap the notes to bring up the playback controls so you can press Play again.

Sort Songs

"Music library" is an apt name for your collection of tunes. The Pre sorts the songs in your library in various ways, so you'll see buttons on the main screen for artists, albums, songs, genres, and playlists (which are explained in the next section). Tap any button to see your music sorted according to that category.

To hear a song, tap its title. You can listen to songs in the order they're listed or tap the Shuffle All button at the top of the screen to hear the songs randomly. You see a thumbnail image of the album cover, if one's available, next to song and album titles.

> **Tip** You can scroll up or down any of these lists to find the item you want. To zero in on a song, artist, album, or genre more quickly, type a search term on the keyboard. The Pre's nifty search smarts narrow your choices each time you press another letter. Tap the item you want when it appears on the list.

Playlists on the Pre

Playlists—a set of songs you compile to reflect a mood or theme—are a staple of MP3 players. You listen to music while doing all sorts of things—enjoying an intimate dinner, attending a frat party, soothing a sobbing infant—and you want playlists that are right for the moment. Unfortunately, you can't create playlists on the Pre, but you *can* add playlists you create on your computer when you sync your Pre with it, as explained on page 181.

Change the Playback Display

When you listen to music, the Pre displays either the song title or the album's cover art. Select the view you prefer by using the icons on the far right of the menu bar at the top of the screen:

- **Playlist view.** In this view, the Pre displays a song's title, how much time has elapsed since the song began, and how much time is left in the song. A progress bar slowly moves across the song title. Tap the track's title to pause the song.

- **Album Art view.** If the song has an album cover associated with it, the Pre displays it in the center of the screen, flanked by the edges of the album covers for the previous and next songs. If there's no album art, the Pre displays a generic cover (musical notes and the picture of a record— you remember records, right?). Flick the album cover left or right to skip to the next or previous song or album.

Name of the playlist or album

Switch to playlist view

Track number/ total tracks in playlist or album

Tip You can change the order of items in the Now Playing roster by tapping and holding a song name and dragging it to a new spot on the list.

Scratch a Song

If you see an upcoming song in a playlist you'd just as soon skip, swipe it off the side of the screen. The song is still on your Pre, but you won't hear it during this listening session. The song returns the next time you open that playlist.

Remove a Song

When you find a song you really can't stand, the only way to completely remove it from the Pre is to get your computer involved. Aside from merely annoying you, the tune may also be hogging space you could use for a more deserving piece of artistry. To ditch a ditty (or a video):

❶ **Connect the Pre to your PC or Mac using the USB cable.**

❷ **Tap USB Drive on the Pre.**

❸ **If you're using a Windows XP PC, open My Computer; if you're on a Windows Vista machine, open Computer.** On a Mac, open the Finder.

❹ **In Windows, use Windows Explorer to delete the song from the Pre.** On the Mac, drag the file to the Trash.

The Pre as Radio

You can treat your Pre as a radio using a free program from the App Catalog called Pandora Internet Radio. Pandora is a music lover's delight: Type in the name of a favorite song, artist, or composer, and Pandora puts together a personalized "radio station" featuring music that matches your taste.

For example, type in *Beatles,* and Pandora features songs from the Fab Four as well as acts with similar music styles. Or type in a classic song title like *Summertime,* and Pandora asks if you want to create a station built around the Ella Fitzgerald version, the Janis Joplin version, or versions by numerous other artists.

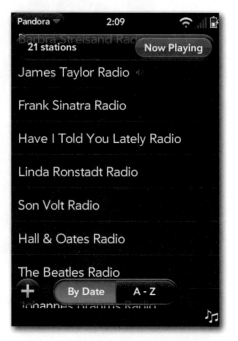

You can help Pandora fine-tune your radio station by tapping the thumbs-up or thumbs-down buttons under the current song's album cover. That tells Pandora what you like and don't like so it can adjust its playlist accordingly.

You can also bookmark songs and artists to learn more about them or to buy their works later. Or you can tap the Buy button to go to Amazon and download the song. Best of all, Pandora can play in the background while you do other things. (The iPhone version of Pandora can't.)

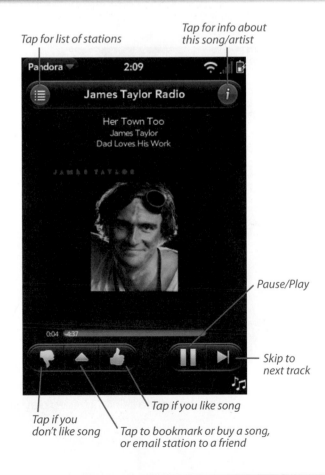

Tap for list of stations

Tap for info about this song/artist

Pause/Play

Skip to next track

Tap if you like song

Tap if you don't like song

Tap to bookmark or buy a song, or email station to a friend

Play Videos

In addition to transferring videos to the Pre, you can add video files to your Pre two other ways: as email attachments or as part of MMS messages (see page 145).

The types of video you can put on the Pre are limited. You can't drag over copy-protected music videos or movies from your computer's iTunes library, and that pretty much eliminates anything with Hollywood box-office appeal. (Come to think about it, it eliminates most other films, too.) Of course, the movies you produce yourself with a camcorder are fair game, as are video podcasts.

> **Note** Here's the geeky list of video formats the Pre plays: MPEG4, H.263, H.264, MP4, 3GP, 3GPP 3G2, and 3GP2. You'll be quizzed on this later (just kidding).

To play videos on the Pre, open the Videos program by tapping its icon, , in the Launcher. The Pre lists all your videos, complete with a thumbnail image from each one.

Tap a video in the list to start playing it. (Videos play back in landscape mode, so turn your Pre on its side.) Tap the screen to bring up video playback controls.

The ▶ and ❚❚ buttons work the same way they do when you're listening to music (page 190). Instead of fast-forward or rewind buttons, however, you move forward or backward in a movie by dragging the slider at the bottom of the playback window in either direction.

Palm also threw in a fancy and less obvious trick for moving forward or backward in a video: Flick the screen from left to right to advance the video by 30 seconds. Flick the other way to rewind it 10 seconds. Tap the ▣ video switch to toggle between full-screen view and the original size.

Note The Pre automatically pauses videos if you press the center button to go into Card view.

Watch YouTube

The Pre includes a program for YouTube, the wildly popular video-sharing site. YouTube is a haven for homegrown videos, but its influence and reach have evolved well past that, as anyone who has watched a political campaign message on the site can attest.

Start by tapping the YouTube icon in the Launcher.

When you first open the program, it lists the most popular videos on the site. Tap the menu bar at the top of the screen to switch to YouTube's most-viewed videos, or to see, via the History list, the videos you recently viewed. If you've got a topic in mind, type a search term in the box near the top of the screen, though it's often more fun to browse aimlessly.

Video listings include a thumbnail movie still along with details like the length of the clip, its user rating, and the number of people who've viewed it. (There's not necessarily a meaningful correlation between viewers and quality, though you can judge for yourself.)

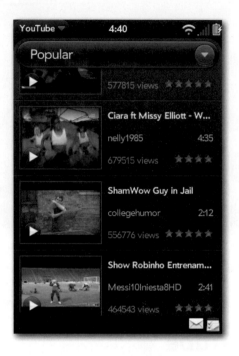

If you're not convinced a video is worth watching, tap the text to the right of the thumbnail for a synopsis. This screen includes two buttons at the bottom: More and Share. Tap More→"More from this Author" to find other videos by the same person or More→Related Videos to find videos with similar content.

Tap a video's thumbnail image to play it. While you're watching, tap the screen to bring up the playback controls. Tap Share to send someone a link to that video via email or text message (the Pre's Email or Messaging program opens automatically).

Watch TV

Sprint TV offers free live and prerecorded TV, subscriber channels, movie rentals, and radio stations. Free live TV includes ABC Mobile, the Disney Channel, and the NFL Network. Free prerecorded TV, which Sprint calls On Demand, includes The Weather Channel, Bravo to Go, and Access Hollywood.

It also offers several for-pay "premium" channels. My Local TV costs $4.95 per month plus tax for the privilege of watching clips from select news outlets across the country. The channel promises to deliver breaking news, plus sports and weather, to your Pre. You can see lists of stations by the states and cities where they're available. Segments are updated several times a day. Kids Zone offers a bundle of channels, including Cartoon Network, National Geographic, and Sesame Street, for $9.99 a month, plus tax. And the Music Video Channel commands $6.95 a month plus tax.

Sprint Movies gives you access to recent releases catalogued by genre (comedy, drama, horror, and so on) and popularity. Rentals cost $4.99 to $5.99 plus tax, and you only have 24 hours to watch them.

Sprint TV also offers assorted free and fee-based radio stations.

The NASCAR Application

Sprint sponsors NASCAR (National Association for Stock Car Auto Racing), so if you're a racing buff, you're in luck. The Pre includes a NASCAR program, where you can watch videos of races, look up driver statistics, get the latest news, and so on.

Chapter

9

The Pre as Camera

The truth about cellphone cameras is that none of them are in the same league as those black, chunky, professional-grade cameras with big lenses (and big price tags). You wouldn't think of using a camera phone to shoot a family portrait, for example, or images of a lunar eclipse. In fact, most cellphone cameras don't even measure up to modestly priced point-and-shoot digital cameras.

But the upside of camera phones is that you almost always have them with you. So they can come in really handy when Junior kicks the winning goal in soccer, when grandma blows out the candles on her 90th birthday cake, and when you get into a fender-bender and need evidence for the insurance company.

This chapter covers the Pre's dead-simple camera. You'll learn how to snap photos, admire and share them, and use your photos as the Pre's background display or as an image that pops up when a friend calls.

Snap Shots

As cellphone cameras go, the Pre's 3-megapixel model stacks up nicely. It takes decent pictures in low light and doesn't have a lot of *shutter lag* (the time between when you press a button to take a picture and when the Pre actually captures the image). As long as you don't expect too much from the Pre's camera (you wouldn't want to use the images it creates as wall-sized posters, for example), you'll be pleased with the results.

But the Pre's camera isn't perfect. You long for an autofocus feature and a zoom lens. It doesn't have any souped-up editing features that let you change a color shot to black and white or sepia-toned. It doesn't have a slideshow feature for photos, and you can't shoot video.

But shooting pictures with the Pre is as easy as using one of those old Kodak Instamatics—except that you don't need to get the film developed.

Capture the Moment

To take a picture, start by tapping the camera icon  in the Launcher. You'll see a picture of a camera onscreen for a second before the display morphs into a viewfinder. A crossbar in the middle of the screen helps you focus on your subject (who should be at least 18 inches away, by the way).

Viewfinder crossbar

Open Photos gallery　　*Take picture*　　*Flash setting*

These buttons appear at the bottom of the screen:

- **Photo gallery.** The leftmost button, 📷, takes you to the Pre's photo gallery, where all the pictures on your Pre live, whether you took them with the camera itself or imported them from elsewhere (see next page).

- **Snap a picture.** The big, green 📷 button in the center triggers the camera's shutter, but it's not the only way to shoot an image: You can also slide out the keyboard and press the space bar. Either way, the Pre plays the sound of a traditional camera's shutter snapping (you can turn this sound off by sliding the ringer switch to off).

> **Tip** This may seem obvious, but always make sure the camera's lens is clean. Use a soft, lint-free cloth to wipe it off.

- **Flash.** Unless you're an experienced photographer, you may not know exactly when to use a flash. If that's the case, leave the flash setting on Auto ᴬᵁᵀᴼ (the default) and let the camera decide.

  If you're sure you want to use the flash, tap the ᴬᵁᵀᴼ button once, and it changes to the ⚡ icon. If you definitely *don't* want the flash to fire—if you're somewhere that prohibits flash photography, say—tap ᴬᵁᵀᴼ twice until you see the 🚫 icon. The flash won't go off in even the darkest of rooms. Tap the button once more to get back to the Auto setting.

> **Tip** In general, the brightest source of light should be behind you. So if you're indoors, don't shoot something that's in front of a lamp or window.

The Steady Cam

To take a photo of cooperative, steady subjects, like mountain ranges and trees, simply tap and release the 📷 button. But for subjects that tend to move around, like kids, dogs, and ocean waves, you can try a few strategies to get blur-free shots.

If you want to shoot something that's moving, you increase the odds of getting crisp results if you press and hold the 📷 button, and then release it only at the moment you want to capture the scene. The camera patiently waits for you to lift your finger before it shoots.

Tip Flip the Pre over when you have the keyboard open to see the mirror on the back of your phone. It can help you straighten your tie or fix your makeup before you take a picture of yourself, but can't help you frame a self-portrait—your face looks big and distorted in it, and you can't make out what's in the background.

You can also try freezing a shot by using the space bar as the shutter key. Slide open the keyboard, steady the camera by holding the Pre with two hands, and then press the space bar to snap an image.

Tip If you hold down the space bar, you'll take a shot every second. It's not exactly rapid fire like some expensive digital cameras, but it's a cool effect if your kid is plunging off a diving board.

Finally, you can try an old standby: brace your body against a wall or other immovable object to steady the camera.

In any of these scenarios, turn your phone sideways to take wide shots (called *landscape mode*). Try these shots with the keyboard open and closed to see which method you find more comfortable.

Tip When you turn the Pre so it's in landscape mode, the three buttons at the bottom of the screen re-orient themselves to either the left or right side of the screen (depending on which way you hold the camera).

Import Pictures

The Pre automatically saves the pictures you take. But there are several other ways to get pictures onto your Pre:

- **Sync pictures** from your PC desktop using iTunes (if this feature is still available; see the Note on page 181). Connect the Pre and your desktop through the Pre's USB cable and choose Media Sync from the buttons that pop up. In iTunes, under Devices, click "Palm Pre" and then click the Photos tab. Click "Select photos from" and choose your photos folder from the drop-down list. Then import "All photos" or "Selected folders." (For a detailed description of syncing media files, see page 181.)

You can pretty much follow the same routine on a Mac. In iTunes, click on "Palm Pre" under Devices in the Source list, then click the Photos tab, and then select the albums or photos you want to import.

- **Copy pictures** from a PC or Mac by connecting the Pre's USB cable to your computer, tapping USB Drive, and then transferring the files as explained on page 184.

- **Receive images** as email attachments or as part of incoming MMS messages (see page 148).

- **Download pictures** from the Web.

> **Note** The Pre can display pictures that arrive as email attachments or in an MMS message if they're in JPG, GIF, BMP, or PNG formats. In the Photos program, you can view pictures that are in JPG format.

Organize Images

All the pictures on your Pre—ones you've taken, imported, or downloaded—end up in the same place: the photo gallery, the Pre's digital shoebox. As explained on page 205, you get to it by tapping the button in the Camera program to launch the Photos application, or by going to the Launcher and tapping the Photos icon.

On the main screen of the Photos application, you see a list of all your existing albums. To the right of each album's name you see three images from that album (assuming there are at least three images in the album), along with a number indicating how many total images the album contains.

The Pre automatically organizes your images into the following albums:

- **All images.** The whole enchilada—your complete photo collection.

- **Photo roll.** All the pictures you took using the Pre's camera.

- **Messaging.** Images that arrive via email or MMS (page 148).

- **Wallpapers.** Your *wallpaper* is the image you see on the screen when you turn on the Pre or that appears in the background when you switch to Card view. The Pre includes a dozen exquisite scenes to use as wallpaper. As you'll learn on page 212, you can use your own pictures as wallpaper, too.

- **Media sync.** An album for the pictures you transfer via iTunes (if that capability is still available; see the Note on page 181).

- **Downloads.** The dumping ground for pictures fetched from the Web.

- **Screen captures.** This is where any pictures you take of what's on the Pre's screen end up. Page 217 tells you how to do that.

Tip The names of some of the Pre's albums are written in all lowercase letters ("downloads", "screencaptures", "wallpapers", and so on). If this bothers you or you want to name your albums something else, connect the Pre to a computer, tap USB Drive, and then change the file names on your PC or Mac.

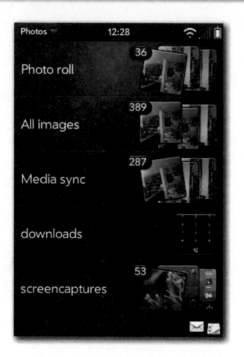

Move Pictures to New Albums

You can move pictures from one album to another and create additional albums, but you can't do either of these tasks on the Pre itself.

Connect the Pre to your computer with the Pre's USB cable (page 184 tells you how), and then create new folders in My Computer on a Windows XP machine, Computer on a Vista machine, or the Finder on a Mac. Here's how:

After you connect the Pre to your computer, open the drive that represents the Pre and find the DCIM folder. (That's geek shorthand for the even geekier Discrete Control Interface Module.) Create a new folder inside the DCIM folder and give it a name like Junior's First Birthday party. That new folder will become an album of the same name in the Pre's Photos app.

Then copy or drag a picture from the folder it resides in on the computer into the new folder. (The folder has to contain at least one image for the Pre to pick it up and make it an album.) When you're done, eject the Pre from the computer, and the new album should be on it.

You can't delete an album directly from the Pre. If you ever want to delete one, you have to connect the Pre to the computer with the USB cable and then, on the computer, delete the appropriate folder from the Pre's DCIM folder.

Manage Pictures

In the Camera program, tap the photo gallery icon , and then tap on an album's name to see all the pics it contains, which pop up 12 at a time as thumbnails. The images all appear on a single screen (instead of spreading out over several pages), so you have to scroll up or down to see more than the first dozen.

View Photos

With an album open, tap an image to zoom in on it. (The picture enlarges right away, but takes a second to come into focus.) A menu bar at the top of the screen tells you the name of the parent album and the picture's number (for example, "Vacation Shots 6/14" means you're looking at the sixth picture out of 14 in the album called "Vacation Shots").

You can manipulate your photos in various ways:

- **Swipe** to the left or the right to move to the next or previous image, respectively. Or drag a picture just far enough to peek at the next or previous image.

Album name — *Picture number/ total images in album*

Photo roll 20/42

- **Double-tap** the screen to zoom in on the spot you tapped. Double-tap again to zoom back out.

- **Pinch-and-spread.** Remember this gesture from Chapter 2 (page 29)? Pinch your thumb and forefinger together, place them on the screen, and spread them apart to magnify an image; move them back together to shrink the image. Pinching gives you more control over exactly what gets magnified than double-tapping, and the effect is a lot more satisfying.

- **Pan by dragging** the image around. Panning only works if you magnify the picture beyond the limits of the screen.

- **Rotate the Pre** 90 degrees to orient landscape shots properly. If you don't, the Pre flanks horizontal images with thick black bars above and below. When you turn the Pre on its side, order is restored and the image fills the screen.

Tip If you flip the Pre over to show a picture to a friend, the screen orients itself properly so the photo is right side up.

Delete Duds

Even if you have Ansel Adams' DNA, you'll take some pictures that just don't work. Maybe one of the kids blinked, or the lighting was less than perfect. Whatever the case, you can't get rid of it fast enough.

To delete a picture, tap the image's thumbnail so it enlarges to full screen and displays the menu bar ⚟ above it. (If the photo is already full-screen, but the menu bar has disappeared, tap the screen to bring back the bar.) Then tap the trash can icon 🗑 at the right end of the bar. If you change your mind, tap the Cancel button that comes up in the next screen; if not, tap the red Delete button. Once a picture is gone, it's gone forever (unless you saved it somewhere other than the Pre). The Pre *doesn't* back pictures up to your Palm Profile.

Delete Image?

This action cannot be undone.

Delete

Cancel

Use a Picture as Wallpaper

Your Pre is one smart-looking gadget, and one reason for that is the drop-dead gorgeous photos Palm supplies as the phone's wallpaper. Because the images are so beautiful, you'll likely stare at the screen an awful lot.

Out of the box, the Pre uses an image of budding orange flowers as the wallpaper. Palm includes 11 other stunning images, but you don't have to use any of them as your wallpaper. After all, what could be more appealing wallpaper than pictures of your loved ones?

To redecorate your phone, go to the Launcher and open the Photos program. Then:

❶ **Open an album and tap a picture to view it full screen.**

❷ **If you want to focus in on just part of the image, double-tap the image to zoom in, and then drag it around to center it on the area you like.**

③ **Tap the screen to call up the menu bar** .

④ **Tap the middle of the menu bar, and then tap "Set wallpaper" in the list that appears.** A Set Wallpaper button appears at the top of the image—tap it to confirm your decision. You'll see a "Setting wallpaper" notification at the bottom of the screen; it changes to read "Wallpaper set" when the job is done.

Assign to contact

Set wallpaper

Share via email

Share via MMS

Upload

Note If you picked one of your own pictures as wallpaper, the Pre doesn't save the image in the wallpapers album.

Set Wallpaper

There's another way to change your wallpaper: Tap the Screen & Lock icon in the Launcher, then tap Change Wallpaper, and then choose a photo from the list of albums that pops up (follow the instructions in the above list). Or tap New Photo at the top of the screen to open the Camera app and snap a picture.

Add Pictures to Contacts

You can assign a picture to a friend's or colleague's profile so that when you call that person or she calls you, her image pops up on your screen. This is a good way to see who's calling you if you haven't assigned her a custom ring-tone (see page 96). Here's how to set it up:

❶ **Open a photo and tap the middle of the menu bar ▣ , and then tap "Assign to contact".**

❷ **When your Contacts list appears, scroll to the person's name, or type in her name to find her by using search (page 79).**

❸ **Tap the person's name.** The photo now takes up the full screen, with a box over it showing the area of the image that will show up in Contacts.

❹ **Drag the image around to center it within the box until it's positioned the way you want it (spread your fingers to zoom in on a headshot).**

❺ **Tap "Set to Contact".** You'll briefly see the message "Setting contact picture", followed by "Contact picture set".

"Map" Your Photos

Your Pre (and most every other digital camera) attaches *metadata* to each image you shoot, which is a fancy way of saying that it records a set of information with each shot. That info can include things like the time and date you took the picture, the aperture and exposure settings, and whether or not you used a flash.

If you turn on Geotag Photos in the Location Services program (see page 171), the Pre records where you took each picture. (As you learned in Chapter 7, the Pre uses GPS, WiFi hotspots, and cell tower info to figure out your location.) It records this info as GPS latitude and longitude coordinates.

If you geotag your pictures, you can view your images by location. On a Windows PC, for example, you can use the free Picasa photo organizer (*http://picasa.google.com*) to plot pictures on a Google Earth map (assuming you have the free Google Earth program installed—see *http://earth.google.com*). From Picasa, tap Tools→Geotag→"View in Google Earth".

On a Mac, iPhoto has a cool feature called Places that lets you use geotag info to search for all the pictures you took in a particular spot. It's a fast way to find vacation pics you snapped at the Eiffel Tower or Grand Canyon. The Places program displays pins on a Google map; click a pin to view the pictures you took there.

You can also geotag photos you post on Twitter (*www.twitter.com*).

Capture Your Pre Screen

If you ever want to share a picture of what's on your Pre's screen—to show a friend your high score on a game, for example, or to share a picture of a web page—you can use one of the Pre's undocumented features: *screen capture,* which lets you shoot a crystal-clear picture of whatever's on your Pre's screen.

To do that, slide out the Pre's keyboard, and do one of the following:

- Hold down the orange and Sym keys at the same time, and then press the P key.

- Hold down the orange key and the Shift key ⬆ at the same time, and then press the P key.

That's it—you just took a screenshot. (You won't hear a camera-shutter sound like you do when you take a picture with the Camera program.) The Pre saves the image in the "screencaptures" album; launch the Photos application to see it.

> **Tip** Because the Pre doesn't play a sound when you take a screenshot, you may think you missed the shot. But before you snap a duplicate, head to the screencaptures album to check. If you do end up with duplicates, you can delete them the same way as you do any other image (see page 211).

Share Photos

From time to time, you have to pull out your phone to show off pictures of your spouse or kids, or that whopper you caught off Catalina Island. Cellphones have taken over the picture-storage role once reserved for wallets (and you can store a heck of lot more pictures on a cellphone than you ever could in a wallet).

But not everyone wants to congregate around your Pre to see pictures, and they don't have to. You've got lots of other ways to share images from your Pre:

- **To email a picture**, tap the middle of the menu bar at the top of a photo, ▣, and then tap "Share via email". The Email program opens with the image already attached and the From box filled in with your email address. Add the recipient's address, a subject, and whatever message you want, and then tap the Send button ✍.

- **To send a picture by MMS,** tap the photo's menu bar, and then tap "Share via MMS". Enter the name or phone number of the recipient, and type in an accompanying message.

- **To upload a picture** to Facebook or Photobucket (www.photobucket. com), first make sure you added your account information. If not, open the Photos program's application menu and tap Preferences & Accounts→Add An Account→Facebook (or Photobucket). Then enter your user name and password, and tap Sign In.

  If you've already set up a Facebook account for your contacts and calendar as discussed on page 58, you're good to go. Tap the image's menu bar, then tap Upload, and tap your Facebook account name. That's all there is to it—the Pre confirms that your picture is on its way, and you can head to your Facebook profile to see it. Uploading to Photobucket works the same way.

At the time of this writing, the Pre can't upload images to other popular photo-sharing sites like Flickr (*www.flickr.com*). For now, you have to email photos to those sites.

Appendix

A

Get Started with the Pre

You've surely taken your new Pre out of its box and started playing with it by now. And if you bought the phone at a Sprint store, a salesperson has likely walked you through the steps for activating it. It's the least the guy could do—it's not like he had to pressure you to buy one.

If you got your Pre by mail and you're new to Sprint (or if you're getting a new wireless phone number), you have to set up the phone yourself, as outlined in this appendix. The process is easy and shouldn't take more than about 15 minutes.

If you're already a Sprint customer and are transferring your existing wireless number to the Pre, your path is slightly different: Stop by Sprint's online activation page at *http://sprint.com/activate*, enter the phone number you're changing, and then follow the onscreen instructions.

If you run into an activation snafu, call Sprint's Customer Service department at 1-888-211-4727.

Choose the Right Service Plan

When you buy a cellphone, you usually consider a couple of factors: the cost of the phone itself *and* what you have to fork over every month for your voice and data plan.

The Pre costs $199.99 after a rebate. That's a subsidized price for committing to Sprint for a 2-year period (the minimum plan length). If you're new to Sprint, you're also responsible for a $36 activation fee. If you bail out of the plan early, you're on the hook for a hefty early termination fee of up to $200. (They get you coming and going.)

But Sprint and Palm are quite generous on the cost of the monthly plans, especially when you consider that all of them come with unlimited text, picture, and video messaging, plus all the data (web browsing, email messaging, and so on) you can handle.

What you really need to ponder is how many minutes you need for making and receiving phone calls. Sprint's least-expensive plan costs $69.99 a month plus tax and gives you 450 anytime minutes. Weekend calls are free, as are calls you make after 7 p.m.

A plan with 900 anytime minutes goes for $89.99 a month (plus tax), and an *unlimited* voice plan that lets you talk to your heart's content costs $99.99 a month.

Family plans are a sweet deal: A 1,500-minute anytime family plan goes for $129.99, and a 3,000-minute plan costs $169.99. (You'll pay an extra $19.99 a month for 3–5 additional lines.) The unlimited family plan commands $189.98 a month, with an additional 3–5 lines going for $89.99 a month.

If you work for a company that's affiliated with Sprint, you might even qualify for a deeper discount. Check with your employer.

All plans include free GPS navigation (see page 175) and free mobile-to-mobile calling (that's when you call other people who use Sprint's cellular network or they call you).

> **Tip** Don't lose any sleep picking a plan. If you need more or fewer minutes, you can change your plan anytime without penalty.

Activate Your Pre

The first time you turn on your Pre (by pressing and holding the power button and waiting patiently for the pulsating Palm logo to disappear), you have to activate it to consummate the device's relationship with Sprint.

At the outset, you'll be asked to tap English or Spanish as your preferred language, and to confirm your selection.

The Pre then confirms with Sprint that you signed up for one of the voice/data plans mentioned above, and then you see the words "Phone Activated" on the screen. At this point, you can tap an icon at the bottom of the screen to make a call—but only to call Sprint Customer Service or 9-1-1.

You're not quite done yet. You have to accept the Terms and Conditions for Palm Services. These spell out the requirements for use of the phone, third-party fees, and other legalese. Tap Accept if you agree, or tap Decline to annul the marriage before it starts.

Supplying Personal Data

On the next several screens, you set up your Palm Profile (page 3), which ensures you get program updates and provides backup and restore services for everything on the phone—programs, files, and the operating system. To set up a Profile, enter your name, choose a password, and supply an email address. Palm sends you a verification email.

At this point, you can choose whether you want to activate the Pre's GPS feature, called *Location Services* (page 170). If so, you have to confirm that you'll adhere to Google's privacy policies; Google collects and aggregates anonymous location data (though you can turn this off—see page 171).

And you probably *will* use Location Services, because you need it for handy features like turn-by-turn driving directions and finding local movie theaters and restaurants. You can choose whether programs that use Location Services can turn it on automatically, or whether they have to ask your permission each time (see page 170).

Before the setup drill is complete, Palm teaches you a few of the most basic finger techniques for interacting with the phone (they're all covered in Chapter 2). After that, tap Restart to apply your settings, and watch your Pre restart. Congratulations—you're now a member of the Pre family.

Appendix

B

The App Catalog

In many respects, the Pre is a groundbreaking device. But it has some serious catching up to do when it comes to the number of programs available for it.

The Pre's online program emporium, called the *App* (short for "application") *Catalog,* offered all of 30 programs as this book went to press. Compare that to the more than *65,000* applications (and counting) in the archrival Apple's App Store for the iPhone and iPod Touch. Even if you flunked math, you can see that's a ginormous difference.

But Apple took more than a year to start selling programs for the iPhone. And Palm says that its App Catalog is still in *beta* (preview mode) and simply not quite ready for prime time. Even a few weeks after the Pre's much-ballyhooed debut in June 2009, the App Catalog was occasionally unavailable, bolstering the company's claim of beta status.

It's unlikely to stay that way. Custom-built programs are vital to any smartphone's future, and the Pre is no exception. The custom apps provide everything from social networking aids (like LinkedIn and Twitter) to straight-out news delivery (from sources like *The New York Times* and the Associated Press).

Palm has a long and successful history with the independent programmers who put these applications together, and you can be sure they'll be writing lots of Pre programs in the days and years ahead. So, eventually you'll be hanging out in the App Catalog a lot. In this brief chapter, you'll learn how to shop the virtual corridors of the Pre's online mall. Don't worry—you won't have to fight for a parking space.

Meet the Mall

The entrance to the App Catalog, as with most Pre programs, is in the Launcher. Tap the App Catalog icon  to get through the door.

In at least one way, the App Catalog is a lot like a real-world "brick-and-mortar" store: It displays sale items prominently. The first screen you see has thumbnails representing featured applications at the top, which at press time included Pandora Internet Radio (page 194), AccuWeather forecasts, and Citysearch (local business listings). Swipe right or left to see more featured programs.

A list of the store's most popular programs follows. They include the FlightView Flight Tracker program, Goodrec's GoodFood restaurant finder, and Handmark's Express Stocks, which lets you track your portfolio.

If you know what you're looking for, search for it by typing its name in the search box at the top of the screen. Tap the magnifying-glass icon or press the Enter key ◀ to start the search. You can also scroll down the main screen to browse programs by program type (Entertainment, Lifestyle, and so on) and by attribute (top-rated and most recent, for example). Eventually, you should also be able to search by price, but for now, most of the programs are free.

Sample of programs in the App Catalog's Business category

Among the most interesting early programs are those tied in with the Pre's GPS smarts:

- **Where** helps you find cheap gas, Starbucks locations, and fellow Where users near you.

- **Fandango** finds movie theaters and displays local show times. You can buy tickets through the Pre, and automatically block out the time on your Pre calendar.

- **Classic** from MotionApps emulates the old Palm operating system on the Pre. This $30 program lets you run many of the programs you bought for earlier Palm products, including the Treo and other, older Palm handhelds. (These older programs are confined to the Classic application and don't interact with newer programs on the Pre.)

Shop Smart

To learn more about an application, tap its listing. You can read user reviews, add your own rating (but only after you buy or download the program), see screenshots, and read a description from the program's creator. You can tap a link to visit the creator's home page and, sometimes, a customer support page, too. Doing either opens the Pre's browser.

Best of all, you can take most apps out for a spin before deciding whether to part with any money. To do that, tap the "Try me" button in the menu bar at the bottom of the screen.

Once you download an application, tap the "Tap to launch" bar at the bottom of the screen to open it. The download process creates an icon for the program in the Launcher.

If an application has an update associated with it, a small, blue arrow icon will appear in the corner of the program's icon. Visit the program's App Catalog page for a link to update details.

Appendix
C

Get Help

I f he were alive today, Dr. Seuss might say this about the Pre: "A computer's a computer, no matter how small." And computers, no matter how small, have problems from time to time.

The Pre, too new to have a track record for long-term reliability, is by all appearances a solid smartphone. So consider this appendix a guide to the little—and big—things that *might* go wrong and what you can do to get out of a pickle.

Update Your Software

From time to time, Palm issues updates to the Pre's operating system, the program that controls the smartphone's basic functions (see page 5), to fix bugs and add features. When that happens, you'll see a note in the Pre's notifications area.

You can tap Install Later to postpone an update, but unless you have a compelling reason to do so, you should install it right away. Palm wouldn't provide one if it weren't important, and you can only put off an update three times. After that, the Pre automatically installs it. So tap Install Now to get it over with and possibly avoid problems the update is designed to fix.

You can manually check for updates by going to the Launcher and tapping Updates. You'll not only see updates to the Pre's operating system (in case you somehow missed a notification), but updates to any third-party programs you own, too.

Battery Issues

Palm estimates that you can charge the Pre's lithium ion battery through 400 to 500 full *cycles.* One cycle means fully draining and then fully charging the battery. But cycles are kind of like mileage on a car: Ten 1-mile trips or one 10-mile trip will increase the odometer reading by the same amount. So it goes with the Pre's battery: If you drain the battery 10 percent and then fully charge it, and repeat that process 10 times, that wears the battery out just as much as draining it 100 percent and then fully charging it does. As the battery gets older, it won't completely fail; it'll just hold less of a charge.

Here are some tips for improving the battery's longevity:

- Switch to Airplane mode (see page 6) to turn off WiFi, phone capabilities, and Bluetooth signals when you're not using them. All of these services drain the battery.

- Set the display to turn off after 30 seconds of inactivity: Tap Screen & Lock in the Launcher, then, in the Screen section, tap "Turn off after" and select "30 seconds". While you're there, make sure the screen's brightness setting is as low as you can bear.

- If you don't get a lot of urgent email messages, you can have the Pre check for email less often. Open Email and go to the application menu. Tap Preferences & Accounts and then tap the name of the account you want to adjust. Scroll down to the Sync section, and tap the Get Email box. Pick a time interval from the list, or choose Manual so you can have the Pre fetch email only when you have time to read it. If the account gets only a few messages a day, the As It Arrives setting is another good way to go. You can also turn off an account's Show Notification switch to prevent the Pre from waking up every time a new message comes in.

- Instant messaging also drains the battery, even if you're signed in but not actively sending messages. If you do a lot of it, plug the phone in.

- Charge the battery as often as possible to avoid a full discharge. It's better to top off the Pre's battery than to fully charge it from scratch.

- Don't charge the battery in direct sunlight or in a humid room. Hot batteries degrade faster, especially if they're fully charged (or close to it).

- If you have a spare battery, keep the metal contacts clean, and don't store it in a hot environment.

Even if you do all of the above, batteries have a finite life—and sometimes they die before their time. You can replace the battery by following the directions on page 22. Palm sells spare batteries for about $50 at *http://palm.com/ us/products/phones/pre/index.html*. You might be able to find cheaper ones online, but be wary of cells that aren't approved by Sprint or Palm—they may void your warranty or damage the phone.

Pulling out the Pre's battery is as good as turning it off, so if you remove the battery, remember to hold down the power button to restart the phone after you put it back in. It's normal for the Pre to take a while, so expect to see the startup Palm logo onscreen for a bit.

Dark Screens

If the Pre's screen seems kind of dim once you turn on the phone, tap anywhere on the screen to brighten it. If you can barely make out the screen after that, go to the Launcher, open Screen & Lock, and then slide the brightness setting up. If you still have a dim screen, plug in the phone; you may have a weak battery.

If the problem persists, restart the phone:

❶ **Tap Device Info in the Launcher.**

❷ **Tap Reset Options (you have to scroll down to see it).**

❸ **Tap Restart.** Just as restarting a PC or Mac sometimes fixes glitches, restarting the Pre can have a similar effect.

Here are a couple of other ways to restart:

- Press and hold down the power button while you turn the ringer switch off and on three times.

- Press the orange key, the Sym key, and the R key at the same time.

Slow Programs

Do you count "One-Mississippi, two-Mississippi, three-Mississippi," and find that a program *still* fails to open? Or is an application open but responding slowly? Unfortunately, occasional sluggishness on the Pre is normal.

But there's sluggish and there's *sluggish.* One solution is to restart the phone as explained in the previous section, but before you do that, press the center button to go into Card view, and then close any open applications you're not using. All running programs stake a claim to some of Pre's most precious resource—memory—so closing unused programs frees up memory for the program you're trying to use.

Frozen Programs

If a program won't respond at all, go to the Launcher, open Device Info (if you can), and restart the phone, as explained on the previous page. If you can't get to Device Info, try Plan B: Hold down the power button, and turn the ringer switch off and on three times to restart the Pre.

Erase and Restore Your Pre

If all else fails, you may have to take drastic measures and *reset* your phone. Resetting means you'll lose some or all of your program files—*unless* you back them up first. So you should manually back up the phone before going any further. (Palm automatically backs up your Pre daily, but if you made changes since the last backup, you don't want to lose them.) By manually backing everything up, when the Pre restores your phone's settings, it also restores all your applications, both included apps, those you downloaded later from the App Catalog, and all of your program files.

The Pre backs up your contacts, calendar events, and tasks to your Palm Profile, along with some system settings and programs you've downloaded. It also backs up your user name and password for Microsoft Exchange, Google, POP email accounts (page 127), and your AIM account (see page 148). For Yahoo and Facebook, it only backs up your user name, so you have to reenter your password (you'll be prompted to do so when you restore everything). And you'll have to resync all these accounts. For a summary of what gets backed up and what doesn't, check out *http://tinyurl.com/lv4p6e*.

To manually back up your data, go to the Launcher and tap Backup, and then tap "Back up now".

Now you're ready to partially or fully erase the info on your phone:

- A **partial erase** removes programs you installed and calendar events, contacts profiles, tasks, and settings. It doesn't remove your files: pictures, videos, music, and documents.

- A **full erase** removes programs you installed and calendar events, contacts profiles, tasks, and settings, just like a partial erase. It *also* removes files you created or downloaded: pictures, videos, music, and documents. But a full erase doesn't remove the information in your Palm Profile: all the info and applications you just backed up. And it doesn't affect information in your synchronized online accounts either (Google, Facebook, and Microsoft Exchange).

To erase your Pre, go to the Launcher and tap Device Info. Scroll down and tap Reset Options, and then tap either Partial Erase or Full Erase. Since erasing info is a big step, you have to confirm your choice by tapping Partial Erase or Full Erase again. (The erase process takes a few minutes.) If you change your mind, tap Cancel.

Following the erase, you have to repeat the Pre setup and activation drill (see page 223) as if this were your first time using the device. The Pre prompts you to choose English or Spanish, and you have to agree to Palm's terms and conditions again. To restore info to your Pre after you do the erase, sign into your Palm Profile with your email address and password on the next screen. Anything you backed up—including programs you bought through the App Catalog—makes a comeback, though it may take a few minutes depending on how much information you restore. After that, tap Done to restart the Pre.

Tip *Don't* create a new Palm Profile. If you do, the Pre will think you're a brand-new owner, and you won't have access to all the stuff you backed up.

After either a full or partial erase, you have to resynchronize your Google, Facebook, and Microsoft Exchange accounts. Page 57 explains how to do that.

Finicky Gestures

Gesture area

Mastering the Pre's gestures takes practice. You may perform the right gestures but in the wrong place, for example, so it's helpful to review where the gesture area begins and ends.

As you learned on page 18, the gesture area is a narrow strip that extends across the front of the Pre from the bottom of the touchscreen to the middle of the center button.

If the Pre isn't cooperating with orders you issue from the gesture area, your fingers might be below the lower edge of the gesture area, so try moving them up a bit.

> **Tip** You can tell when you've got your finger in the gesture area because the center button lights up.

Remember that some finger motions aren't confined to the gesture area. Gestures can start on the touchscreen and end in the gesture area, or start in the gesture area and end on the touchscreen. See page 26 for a gesture refresher.

If you have problems with the back gesture (page 27), you may have turned on Advanced Gestures in Screen & Lock (see page 31). If so, try a shorter left-to-right backstroke across half the gesture area.

Tip If you move your finger from side to side in the gesture area, hidden lights flanking the center button light up one at a time and the center button itself lights up. If you drag your finger up from the gesture area toward the touchscreen or down from the touchscreen into the gesture area, *both* lights light up at once, and the center button also lights up.

Weak Coverage

Cellphone coverage isn't the same everywhere. You may know precisely where along your morning commute the signal drops out, for example. If you experience dropped calls or bad call quality, try the following:

- Move around. Remarkably, moving as little as a foot can make a difference between no signal strength and a few bars' worth. (Remember, white bars in the upper-right corner of the Pre's screen indicate signal strength—you can get five bars max.)

- If you're indoors, move near a window.

- If you have metal window blinds and they're closed, open them. They're not exactly missile shields, but they can wreak havoc on cell signals.

- If you're outside, move away from tall buildings, tall trees, and power lines, all of which can block cell signals.

- If you're a passenger in a car, hold the Pre so it's level with a window.

Connection Problems

If you can't make or receive calls, send or receive text messages or emails, or surf the Web, make sure Airplane mode is off (see page 6).

Other things to try:

- If you've got the Pre connected to your computer in USB Drive mode, disconnect it.

- Restart the phone (page 236).

Echo, Echo

If you're on a call and the person on the other end hears an echo:

- Lower the Pre's volume by pressing the lower-volume button on the side of the phone.

- Hold the phone closer to your ear; sometimes the Pre's microphone picks up sound emanating from the tiny speaker on the front of the phone.

- If you're using the speakerphone feature, turn the Pre over so that it's face-down.

If you're on a call and you hear your *own* voice:

- Ask the other person to lower the volume on his phone.

- Ask him to hold the phone closer to his ear.

Be Heard

If the other person has trouble hearing you:

- Position the microphone closer to your mouth. The mic is that tiny hole below the gesture area (see page 12), so be careful not to cover it with your cheek or chin.

- If possible, try moving to an area with better coverage.

Bluetooth Static

If there's a lot of static on the line, you or the person you're talking to may be in an area with spotty cell coverage (see the previous page for tips on finding a better signal). Or, if you're using a Bluetooth headset (page 97), the headset could be the culprit. In that case, try the following:

- Move closer to the Pre. Despite claims that Bluetooth works at a range of 30 feet, the closer you are to the Pre, the better the signal. Nearby cordless phones and microwaves can also cause interference.

- Check the headset's battery level. If it's low, switch to using the Pre the old-fashioned way: holding it up to your ear.

> **Tip** If you lose the connection between the Pre and a Bluetooth device, "un-pair" the
> devices (see page 100), and then pair them up again (page 98).

Free Up Space

The Pre comes with 8 gigabytes of memory. So if you have a lot of videos, pictures, music, and programs, you'll run out of memory quickly. To check how much memory is still *available,* go to the Launcher and open Device Info.

Preferences ⬇	2:51	📶 📶 🔋

ⓘ Device Information

NAME

Ed Baig's Pre ⌃ ⟩
⌄
◉

PHONE

PHONE NUMBER	
BATTERY	28%
MEMORY	8 GB
AVAILABLE	1.6 GB
VERSION	Palm webOS 1.0.2

✉

If there's not much memory left, free up space by:

- Moving some of your files (old videos or photos, for example) to your computer through Media Sync (if available; see the Note on page 181) or USB Drive mode (see page 184).

- Deleting files you don't need. You can delete images directly on the Pre (see page 211). For other kinds of files, you have to connect the Pre to your computer using Media Sync or USB Drive mode.

- Deleting old emails. Remember, when you delete an email message, it first moves to a deleted-mail folder (the exact name of the folder depends on the account; it could be called Trash, Deleted, or something else). To *permanently* delete a message, remove it from the deleted-mail folder; page 140 tells you how.

- Clearing your web history, cookies, and cache as described on page 169.

- Deleting programs you rarely use (see next section).

Program Problems

Palm advises you to be careful about installing third-party programs that manage ringtones, caller ID applications, instant messages, or that otherwise control your phone's wireless connections. If your phone acts up after you install a new program, try the following, in order:

1. **Restart the Pre.**

2. **Check to see if the company that created the application has issued an update:** Go to the Launcher and tap Updates (see page 50 for more details).

3. **Remove new applications one by one:** Delete the one you installed most recently first, then the second most recent one, and so on. To delete an application, press and hold the orange key on the keyboard and tap the program's icon, and then tap Delete.

4. **Alternatively, go to the Launcher, open the Launcher's application menu, and then tap List Apps.** Find the program you want to remove, tap it, and then tap Delete. (If you decide not to delete a program, tap Done instead of Delete.)

5. **If removing the program solves the problem, get in touch with the program's publisher to see if they have a solution, especially if you paid for the application.**

6. **Install any system-wide updates if you haven't already done so (go to the Launcher and tap Updates).** See page 49 for details.

7. **Perform a partial erase as described on page 237.** This can sometimes fix things if the problem was caused by corrupted data from a third-party program, because it'll delete that bad data.

8. **Perform a full erase as described on page 237.** Again, this gets rid of corrupted data from a problem application.

9. **If the problem appears to be fixed, try reinstalling the programs you removed one by one.** If the problem recurs after you reinstall an application, get in touch with the company that created it.

Passwords and Security

Passwords are frustrating: Every expert says that complex passwords are better because they're harder to crack, but often *you're* the one who ends up locked out. Still, if you're concerned about security and don't want to let just anybody pick up your Pre and see everything that's on it, you'll want to set up a password to protect your info from prying eyes.

You have a choice between two different kinds of passwords for the Pre (one is technically a number). Whichever one you pick, you'll have to enter it each time before you can unlock the screen. Go to the Launcher and tap Screen & Lock, and then scroll down to the Secure Unlock section and tap the word "Off". You'll see a menu that includes the options Simple PIN and Password. If you tap Simple PIN, the Pre lets you set up a 4-digit personal identification number; that's the less secure option. Or you can tap Password and type in a password using the keyboard; the password can be as long as you want and include numbers and letters.

If you forget your Secure Unlock PIN or password, you'll have to reset your phone from a PC. Go to *http://palm.com/support* and enter your Palm Profile email address and password, and then click Wipe Device to remotely reset your Pre (you don't have to have the Pre connected to the computer). Then turn on your phone and sign into your Palm Profile. Any backed up information gets restored, though you'll have to set up your online accounts again.

> **Tip** If your Pre is stolen and you have little hope of getting it back, you should remotely wipe the device so the bad guys can't get your information.

Troubleshooting Tests

At some point, you may encounter a problem so severe that you have to reach out to Palm or Sprint for help. A tech support agent may ask you to run some diagnostic tests.

The Pre includes two kinds of tests: quick and interactive. To get to either, go to the Launcher and tap Device Info→More Info (which you have to scroll down to see). Tap the application menu, and then tap either Quick Tests or Interactive Tests.

The Quick tests include four tests: Memory, WiFi, Bluetooth, and Modem. Despite it being a "quick" test, the memory test takes several minutes to run. The other three tests actually do run quickly.

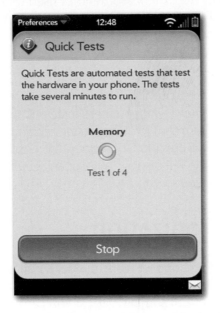

The Interactive tests help diagnose problems with the keyboard; the Pre's other buttons; the touch, proximity, and rotation sensors; the screen and gesture area, speakers, battery, and chargers; and the GPS receiver. When the tests are completed, the agent may ask you to send the results to him by tapping the Send Results button at the bottom of the screen.

Certificates

Certificates are digital documents sometimes used to authenticate informa-tion on a network. For example, your employer might have to issue you a certificate before the Pre can access the company's Exchange servers. (If you have trouble connecting to your office's Exchange server, the certificate could be the problem.) You may also need a certificate to connect to certain WiFi networks.

To troubleshoot a problem with your certificate—if, say, you're working with your company's IT department to diagnose the problem—go to the Launcher and tap Device Info→More Info. Then open the application menu and tap Certificate Manager. The Pre displays a list of any certificates you installed or that were installed by your company.

Sick Synchronization

If you use Microsoft Exchange for work and get a notification that ActiveSync encountered a problem on the server, it's likely a temporary problem. If it persists, check with your IT administrator. If you can't reach the server at all, you may have lost your wireless connection, or the server may be temporarily overwhelmed.

If you have problems synching a single item between your Pre and Exchange and see a notification to that effect, you may have to delete that one item from the Pre.

If you get a notification that there's not enough free memory to synchronize, press the center button to go into Card view, and see how many programs you have running; close any you're not using.

Email Snags

If you're not getting email, the first thing to check is whether you have a con-nection: Look at the status bar (page 14) to see if you have a WiFi or phone signal, and how strong the signal is.

If you do have a signal, then make sure you entered your user names and passwords correctly when you set up the account: Open Email, then go to the application menu and tap Preferences & Accounts→Accounts, and tap the name of the account you're having trouble with. Scroll to the bottom of the screen, tap Change Login Settings, and make sure you entered everything correctly.

Other problems are harder to diagnose. If you suspect the issue has to do with Sprint or the company that provides your email account, call customer service and work through the problem with them.

There are several possible causes and fixes for email problems. Your Internet provider may ask you to install an upgrade to help your WiFi network work with the Pre. There may also be a temporary snag with your provider—all you can do then is wait it out.

It's also possible your email provider has changed some settings; that's likely the case if your email was working just fine and then suddenly stopped working. Or maybe you changed your password for an online email account from a computer, but forgot to make the same change on the Pre.

You can also try doing a partial reset of the Pre (see page 237). That may fix an under-the-hood problem having to do with how the Pre checks for new email.

If you can *receive* email but can't send any, there may be an issue with your authentication setting, which controls outgoing mail. (This setting has a supergeeky acronym—*ESMTP*—which stands for Extended Simple Mail Transfer Protocol, not that there's anything simple about it.) You may also have to change the settings for the outgoing mail server. You'll have to get these settings from your email provider or your company's IT department, and then go into the email account's settings on the Pre and apply any changes (see page 131).

Web Woes

If the Pre can't connect to the Internet, check your connection (page 14). If you can't connect to specific websites or play a video at a site, the problem may be that the Pre's browser isn't compatible with the technologies those sites use—things with names like Flash, Shockwave, VBScript, and WML script. In that case, you're out of luck: You simply can't visit that site on your Pre.

It's also possible that things like secure financial sites won't let you use certain features of the site on the Pre for security reasons. You'll have to use a computer for that site.

Warranty

The Pre comes standard with a 1-year limited warranty. During that 1-year period, Sprint typically manages troubleshooting, exchanges, and repairs in a retail store or by contacting customer service, though Sprint may occasionally pass you along to Palm. All parts and accessories, including the battery, are covered under the warranty, assuming normal wear and tear. A cracked or scratched touchscreen isn't covered, though, nor are scratches on the case.

The cost of an out-of-warranty repair is $199—ouch.

If you want additional protection, you can sign up for Sprint's Total Equipment Protection program. It costs $7 a month, and you have to sign up within 30 days of activating your Pre. The plan covers mechanical and electrical failures, failures due to normal wear and tear, physical damage, loss or theft, and corrosion or liquid damage. Even if you pay for this program, you'll have to pay a $100 deductible to replace your Pre if it's lost or stolen.

Where Else to Turn

Application menus are a good place to find help with basic program operation. For example, when you tap Help in the application menu of the messaging program, you find the basic steps for sending and receiving instant messages. If you don't find what you need there, try one of these options:

- **Call Palm.** The company offers a free 90-day hotline (1-866-750-PALM) for help in setting up your Pre. After that, help costs $14.95 per "incident." (The fee is waived if the call results in an authorized repair that's covered by the warranty.)

- **Call Sprint.** The number is 1-888-211-4727, or you can dial *2 on the Pre.

- **Palm Support Page** (http://tiny.cc/T0Hsu). The Pre support page has guides, tutorials, downloads, and more.

- **Sprint Support Page** (*http://tiny.cc/vVQCG*). Sprint's Pre eLearning Center has troubleshooting guides, tutorials, user reviews, and more.

- **Palm Pre Forum** (*http://palmpreforum.org/*). This is an independent site with forums, reviews, tips, and more.

- **Pre Central** (*http://www.precentral.net*). This site offers guides to Pre features, reviews, forums, and a store for accessories.

Index

drag (gesture), 28, 118, 211
due dates, for tasks, 120–121
duration, of events, 111–113

E

earbuds, 87, 98, 189
early termination fee, 222
earpiece location, 12
echo, minimizing, 90, 241
editable text, 45
editing. *See also* changing
  bookmarks, 167
  email account information, 131
email accounts. *See also* email messages
  account information, editing, 131
  closing, 131
  combining, 68
  customizing, 129–130
  merging, 131–133
  names for, 129
  preferences, 129–130
  reordering, 133
  setting up, 126–128
  syncing, 138
email messages, 126–144. *See also* email
    accounts; folders
  adding sender to contacts, 140
  attachments, adding, 136–137
  attachments, opening, 143–146
  composing, 133–137
  deleting, 140–141, 242
  dialing from, 82
  drafts, 136
  flagging, 142
  forwarding, 140
  gestures while reading, 138
  help guide on, 246–247
  mark as read or unread, 142
  multiple recipients, 134–135
  notifications, 129
  organizing, 141–142
  photos as attachments, 207
  priority, setting, 135
  reading, 137–138
  replying to, 139

sending, 93, 135, 247
sharing photos via, 217
typing, 135
viewing details of, 142
work email, 129
emergency calls, 82–83
erasing and restoring Pre, 237–239
erasing information, remotely, 3
ESMTP (Extended Simple Mail Transfer
    Protocol), 247
EvDo network (Sprint Mobile
    Broadband), 15, 154–155
events, 108–117
  all-day, 116
  annual, 114
  calendar, choosing, 109–110
  calendar, combined vs. separate, 117
  deleting, 117
  detail screen, 112
  duration, 111–113
  future, 110–111
  locations, 113
  meeting requests, responding to, 116
  notes, 116
  notifications, with locked screen, 8
  recurring, 114, 117
  reminders, 114–116
  saving, 110
  time intervals for, 113
  by timeslot, 110
  weekly, 114
Exchange. *See* Microsoft Exchange
Express Stocks (portfolio tracker), 227

F

Facebook
  calendar syncing, 67–68
  contacts, removing, 66
  uploading photos to, 218
family service plans, 222
Fandango (application), 228
Fast Forward button (music), 191
favorite folders (email), 133
favorites list (Sprint Navigation), 175
Features guide, 2
features overview, xv–xvi

L

landscape mode
  for camera, 206
  screen orientation and, 21
  status bar in, 14
  for viewing photos, 211
language setting, 20
latch, back-cover, 10
Launcher. *See also* opening
  adding web pages to, 164–165
  closing, 35
  moving icons in, 34
  opening, 33
  programs available in, 19–21
  removing contacts from, 66
  removing web pages from, 165
  screens in, 34
  using, 33–42
left-to-right swipe, 28
licensing agreements, 2
light direction, for photos, 205
lights, around center button, 38, 240
light sensor, 21
linking contact profiles, 62–63
links in web browsing, 163
listening to voice mail, 89
lists, scrolling through, 28
locations
  for events, 113
  GPS, 169–170
Location Services, 169, 223
locking special character mode
    (keyboard), 42

M

Macs
  copying media files from, 184–185
  syncing with, 69–70
mailer, recycling, 3
main screen (in touchscreen), 13. *See
    also* touchscreen
making phone calls, 74–85
  9-1-1 calls, 82
  automated dialing, 77, 101–102

  dialing by contact, 79, 101
  dialing from web page or email, 82,
      163
  dial pad dialing, 76, 101–102
  hands-free calling, 86–89
  intra-office dialing, 83–84
  keypad dialing, 74–75
  overseas calling, 84–85
  speed dialing, 81–82
  tone preferences, 101
managing multiple calls, 91–92
managing photos, 209–218
  deleting, 211–212
  mapping, 215
  screen captures, 217
  sharing, 217–218
  viewing, 210–211
  wallpaper, using photos as, 212–214
manual actions
  backups before resetting, 237
  email retrieval, 235
  network settings updates, 102
  profile linking, 62
  program updates, 50
  syncing, 65
  syncing with PC, 70
  system updates, 234
mapping photos, 215–216
maps. *See also* Google Maps
  3-D option, 177–178
  centering on current location, 170
  panning, 170
media, 181–199. *See also* photos
  copying files from computer, 182–183,
      184–185
  MP3 player, 189–194
  music from Amazon MP3, 186–189
  NASCAR Channel, 200
  playlists, 192
  radio, 194
  storage capacity for, 189
  TV, 199–200
  videos, 194–195
  YouTube, 197–199
Media Sync, 182
meeting requests, 116, 140

notifications, 48–49. *See also* reminders
  alarms, 48
  area for, in touchscreen, 13, 17
  email messages, 129
  ignored calls, 88
  IMs, 151
  incoming calls, 86
  missed calls, 87
  notifications dashboard, 49
  reordering, 49
  vibrate mode, 97
  voice mail, 88

O

On Demand TV, 199
online accounts
  Palm Profile and, 64
  profiles deleted from, 66
on/off button, 5–6
opening
  App Catalog, 226
  Calendar program, 106
  email attachments, 143–145
  Launcher, 33
  programs, 32, 39
  program's command menu, 40
open networks, 156, 157–158
operating system, 5
  updates, 234
orange key (on keyboard), 42, 44
order, changing. *See* reordering
organizing email messages, 141–142
Outlook, 69, 122
overseas calling, 84–85

P

pairing, with Bluetooth device, 98–100,
    242
Palm Desktop, 69
Palm Pre. *See* Pre
Palm Pre Forum, 249
Palm Profile (calendar)
  as default calendar, 119
  online profile information stored in, 64

Palm Profile (identity), 3–4, 237
  setting up, 223
Palm support page, 249
Palm Synergy. *See* Synergy
Pandora Internet Radio, 194–196, 226
panning, 163, 170
paperclip button (messages), 136
partial erase, 237
passcodes and passwords
  help guide on, 244
  unlocking screen, 7
  voice mail, 89
pasting text, 45–46
Pause button (music), 190
PC
  copying media files from, 182, 184
  copying ringtones from, 96
  syncing to, 68–70
PDF files, 20, 144
PDF View application, 20, 144
phone, 73–103
  advanced settings, 101–103
  features, 90–91
  hands-free calling, 97–101
  incoming calls, 85–89
  keypad dialing, 101
  making calls, 74–85
  multiple calls, 91–92
  multitasking during calls, 91–92, 155
  preferences, 101–103
  ringtones, 93–97
  silencing, 97
phone numbers, in web pages, 163
Photobucket, 218
Photo gallery button, 205
Photo roll album, 207
photos, 209–218. *See also* camera;
    media
  adding to contacts, 214–215
  albums, 207–209
  deleting, 211–212
  downloading from Internet, 207
  file formats, 147
  geotagging, 170
  mapping, 215–216
  metadata for, 215

IP configuration, 158
menu, 41
status bar indicator, 15
syncing with PCs using, 69
for web browsing, 155–159
Wikipedia searches, 47
Windows computers, copying media
files from, 184–185
wipes, remote, 3, 244
wired headset, answering calls while
wearing, 87
wireless. *See* WiFi (wireless) networks
wireless features. *See* Airplane mode;
Bluetooth

Word documents, as email attachments,
144
work email, 129

Y

YouTube, 197–199

Z

zooming
using double-tap, 30
using pinch-and-spread, 29
for web pages, 162

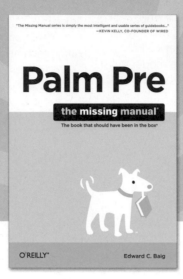

70502